1 MONTH OF
FREE
READING

at

www.ForgottenBooks.com

By purchasing this book you are
eligible for one month membership to
ForgottenBooks.com, giving you
unlimited access to our entire
collection of over 1,000,000 titles via
our web site and mobile apps.

To claim your free month visit:

www.forgottenbooks.com/free892552

ISBN 978-0-266-80791-9
PIBN 10892552

For support please visit www.forgottenbooks.com

CHURCH AND CHAPEL, 1901

MANUAL

and

HISTORICAL SKETCH

of

The First Congregational

CHURCH

Marblehead, Mass.

1684 to 1901

MANUAL

and

HISTORICAL SKETCH

of

The First Congregational

CHURCH

Marblehead, Mass.

1684 to 1901

N. A. LINDSEY & CO..
PRINTERS,
Marblehead, Mass.

Historical Sketch.

A S early as 1635 there seems to have been an attempt made to have preaching in Marblehead. "Rev. John Avery and twenty-one persons, including his family, while on a voyage from Newbury to Marblehead, in one of Mr. Allerton's fishing vessels, were lost by shipwreck, August 15, 1635, on what is known as Thatcher's Island." Mr. Avery was on his way to become the minister of this people. In 1639 there appears to have been preaching, from the record, February 15, that three acres of land were granted by the Salem authorities to Rev. William Walton "to build upon." Nine years later, October 8, 1648, we find the following entry, which is believed to be the first recorded act of the people of Marblehead. "At a town meeting it was agreed on, that there might be an equal way of maintaining the ordinances by Mr. Walton that there should be a rate made, whereby every inhabitant should be rated according to equity; as also strangers, as have benefit by the plantation, by fishing, and make use of wood and timber and enjoy the benefit of the ordinances should be rated according to the discretion of the raters : also to add to every man's rate eighteen pence for Mr. Walton's wood : —and it is agreed that Mr. Walton shall have for this year the sum of *forty pounds.*" In the records for the same year we find it "Ordered, that the rate for the *meeting house* shall be gathered. " It is understood that the meeting house was originally placed on what is now known as the "Old Hill, " near where the ministers are buried. " In 1656 the whole amount raised by taxation was 67 pounds—60 pounds of which was for Mr. Walton's salary, and 40 shillings allowed to Francis Linford for ringing the bell, warning the town and keeping the meeting house clean. " In 1659 "at a general town meeting it was agreed that the meeting house should be seated and a person was employed to complete the work for nineteen pounds. " The following year a committee was appointed " for the placing and seating of all the inhabitants of the town both men and women in the meeting house. " In 1662 it was determined " that a gallery should be built at the North West end of the meeting house, sufficient for four seats, which seats were to be completed, the front seats with columns and a board at the bottom to keep the dust from coming down, and to be arched sufficient to strengthen the meeting house. " " In 1665 it was agreed with John Stacey and Robert

Knight to board the western end of the meeting house from top to bottom and the foreside of the same, also the roof of the meeting house, providing the boards can be obtained." In 1668, "Voted and agreed with Robert Knight, Francis Collings and Jeremiah Neal to build a gallery in the North East end with five seats, stairs and all other necessaries as the other gallery now is," and a person was employed "to look after the meeting house and ring the bell, and officiate about that work, for which he was to have four pounds by the year." Mr. Walton continued to officiate until he was removed by death in August or September 1668. He was succeeded in a few weeks by Mr. Samuel Cheever. At a town meeting held April 6, 1672, it was "Ordered by general consent that a *lentoo* should be built adjoining the back side of the meeting house twenty foot in breadth and forty foot in length, with three gable ends in the same, with timber work." The next year a committee was appointed "to seat the *lentoo* men and women in their seats, put an alley through the old part, dispose of any who should want seats, or lose their seats by means of the alley, in the most convenient place in the old or new part, and rectify any disorders with due care, that such as had been formerly seated, might keep their places, as many of them as conveniently could." "Each person was commanded to retain and use the seat assigned them under a penalty of five pence for each offence." In 1678 "Voted to pay Mr. Cheever's salary 70 pounds *in money.*" In 1679 "Robert Knight was released from paying his town rates during his life for his workmanship in the meeting house in building the gallery." In 1681 "one shilling was paid for an hour glass." The record does not tell when the meeting house was removed from the "Burial Hill" to what is now Franklin Street. It was probably removed between the years 1697 and 1701. It was enlarged at different times, and used there until the erection of the present Stone Church in 1824.

In the year 1684 it was thought desirable by the Christian people residing here, "after serious advice and deliberation" to be organized into a particular church and society; and a unanimous vote to that effect was passed the 6th of August at a regular meeting, at which time it was also voted to invite Mr. Cheever to become their pastor. Mr. Cheever having signified his acceptance of this invitation, and preliminary measures having been taken, the First Church of Christ in Marblehead was regularly organized on the 13th day of August, 1684, consisting of fifty-four members, and Mr. Samuel Cheever was ordained its pastor. "Mr. Higginson of Salem gave him his charge, Mr. Hubbard of Ipswich the right hand of fellowship and both of them, with Mr. Hale of Beverly, laying on of hands : the whole work countenanced with the presence of the Deputy-Governor with five of the assistants, and twenty elders with other ministers and young scholars and many others." Mr. Cheever continued as their pastor, until his death, which occurred May 29, 1724, having preached to them fifty-five years. The last eight of which he had the assistance of a colleague, Rev. John Barnard, who preached for the first time to this people July 11, 1714. Having received an invitation by vote of the church and of the town to become assistant pastor, he accepted, but was not ordained till July 18, 1716—(three months previous to which four males and twenty-four females were dismissed from this church, to form the Second Congregational Church). When Mr. Barnard was installed by a council, consisting of Dr. Cotton Mather, Dr. Colman and others, there were one hundred and seventeen members of this church, twenty-seven males and ninety females. "Honored for his learning and talents, he labored in this part of the vineyard fifty-five years," till removed by death January 24, 1770, in his eighty-ninth year, after Mr. Whitwell had been settled with him eight years. He preached his last sermon January 8, 1769. Mr. William Whitwell received ordination as colleague August 25, 1762, and continued his faithful labors as pastor of this church till his death, November 8, 1781, in the forty-fifth year of his age. January 1, 1783, Mr. Ebenezer Hubbard was ordained pastor, and having held that office less than eighteen years, was suddenly removed by death October 15, 1800, aged forty-three years. Rev. Samuel Dana was ordained October 7, 1801. During his ministry the church and society were blessed with unusual prosperity. There were 480 persons added to the church. . In May of the year 1817, Mr. Dana organized a Sunday School in the Old Meeting House, " for the instruction of poor children and such others as might attend, " which was continued through the summer and till late in the autumn of the same year. June, 1818, the " Marblehead Sunday School Union " was organized, with Hon. William Reed as President, in which this church joined, and the Sabbath School reopened June 14, with Nathan Bowen, superintendent, fourteen male and twenty-three female teachers. The " Union " held its organization until 1829 by which time all of the other schools in town had withdrawn from the Union and left this school an independent organization.

The Chapel on Pearl Street was erected by the church and completed August 18, 1818. And also the " Stone Meeting House, " which was " commenced building in 1824, the walls and roof were completed in November of the same year, the work inside was finished and the house dedicated, July 21, 1825. " Rev. Samuel W. Cozzens was ordained and installed colleague August 8, 1832. Mr. Dana and Mr. Cozzens were dismissed by council at their own request, April 18, 1837.

Rev. Mark A. H. Niles was installed pastor August 30, 1837, and was dismissed November 27, 1844.

Rev. Edward A. Lawrence was installed April 23, 1845, and continued his labors with this church till he received a call to a Professorship in East Windsor Theological Seminary, when he resigned and was dismissed July 12, 1854.

Rev. Benjamin Russell Allen from South Berwick, Maine, was installed November 8, 1854. During his ministry, in 1859, there were about forty members of this church dismissed who were organized into a Third Congregational Church of this town. April 26, 1868, the "meadow lot" given to the church by Rev. Mr. Barnard at his death in 1770, and the "two cows leases" given by William Hayden to the church for the use of the pastor, were sold for $844.59, to which was added about $1,800 by donations, and about $2,200 by the Ladies' Parish Society, with which the lot on High Street was purchased and the parsonage erected. The parsonage was completed, and occupied by Mr. Allen about the last of December, 1869, where he died suddenly June 2, 1872.

John H. Williams of Dudley, a student in Andover Theological Seminary, preached the first time to this people December 22, 1872, and was ordained and installed September 3, 1873.

Following the great fire of June 25, 1877, in which

the meeting house of the Third Congregational Church was burned, that church before dissolving gave letters of dismission and recommendation to this church to fifty-five of her members, all of whom were cordially received.

During the summer of 1878 the question of building a new chapel was agitated, the chapel on Pearl street which for sixty years had served the church with various degrees of satisfaction, was found to be too small for the regular meetings of the church.

Early in the fall of that year, it was voted to purchase the lot on the southerly side of the church and build thereon a chapel of suitable size and containing such convenience as would enable the church to carry on its work more successfully and also to give good accommodation for the regular sessions of the Sunday-school.

Plans for the new chapel were made by Daniel Appleton and a contract was made with John G. Broughton to execute the same. The building was completed and furnished during the winter, at a cost of $4,960.67 and was dedicated March 12, 1879.

A Young People's Society of Christian Endeavor was organized September 22, 1882, with about twenty-five members.

In January, 1883, Rev. Mr. Williams resigned to accept a call to the Clyde Congregational Church, Kansas City, Mo. He preached his farewell sermon February 4, 1883.

Rev. S. Linton Bell preached for this church the first time November 19, 1883, and after a few weeks' service, was invited to become its pastor. He accepted the invitation and was installed February 28, 1884.

In December, 1882, at a business meeting of the church, it was voted that this church ought, in some public and appropriate way, to celebrate the two hundreth anniversary of its organization, occuring August 13, 1884.

A committee was appointed to nominate a Committee of Arrangements for the celebration.

In April, 1884, that committee submitted to the church a list of various names of persons for committees and sub-committees, to make all of the necessary arrangements for the exercises of that celebration.

The report was adopted, and August 13, 1884, was successfully and appropriately celebrated ; a full account of which is to be found in the " Bi-Centennial," published by vote of the church at that time.

On the 13th day of March, 1886, Sarah B. Fettyplace, administratrix of the estate of Lucy C. D. Fettyplace, in behalf of the heirs to that estate, as a memorial to their sister Lucy, presented to the society $5,000, to be used in repairing the stone meeting house.

The gift was accepted.

At a meeting of the society called to consider

the necessity of extensive repairs on the meeting house and act on the report of a committee who had previously been appointed to examine the same, that committee reported the front wall unsafe and should at once be rebuilt, and the floor of the audience room to be so decayed as to require that more than half of it should be made new, and made the following recommendations :

First. Take down the front wall of the church to four feet below the present grade, rebuild the same using the granite, so much of it as is found to be suitable, supplying the deficiency with new granite, and line the entire front wall with brick. New doors and frames to be set three feet and nine inches lower than the present doors, with arched tops and recessed to swing outward, and also new windows and frames with arched tops.

Second. Remove the embankment on the front of the church to the depth of five steps and rebuild the embankment wall and cap it with granite.

Third. The front half of the vestibule floor to be lowered to the level of the doors, and six steps made from each door to the landing, with suitable posts, rails and balusters.

Fourth. Remove all of the pews and the pulpit, take out so much of the floor and timbers as are found to be decayed and replace with new. The pews to be reset with four aisles instead of three as at present. Make an orchestra platform on the right of the pulpit, and supply all needed material.

By a unanimous vote the report was accepted and the recommendations adopted. The following were made a committee to contract for and superintend the work : Nathan P. Sanborn, John Pitman, William Neilson, William Stacey and Isaac M. Munroe. The committee contracted with Messrs. Parsons & Peterson of Salem to do the mason work and with John G. Broughton to do the carpentry work.

The work of taking down the front wall was begun May 10, and the removing of the pews June 1, 1886.

In taking down the wall, back of the stone over the center door on which the date was marked, there was found, embedded in the mortar, a silver plate about four inches wide and five inches long, with the following inscription engraved upon it :

" THIS TEMPLE

" for the worship of Jehovah Father Son and
" Holy Ghost in the first church in Marble-
" head constituted August 13, 1684, was
" erected A. D. MDCCCXXIV Samuel Dana
" pastor ; under the direction of William
" Reed, Calvin Briggs and Dan Weed, agents
" of the society, principally by the munifi-
" cence of individuals and more than all
" others of Hon. William Reed.

Laus Deo !

(Reverse Side.)
" Ministers of the Society
" 1.   John Avery 1635
" 2.   William Walton officiated 30 years, and
" died 1668
" 3.   Samuel Cheever after preaching 16
" years, ordained first pastor August 13, 1684
" died May 29, 1724 Æt 85
" 4.   John Barnard ordained colleague pastor
" July 18, 1716 died January 24, 1770 Æt 89
" 5.   William Whitwell ordained colleague
" Aug. 25, 1762 died Nov. 8, 1781 Æt 45
" 6.   Ebenezar Hubbard ordained Jan. 1,
" 1783 died Oct. 15, 1800 Æt 43
" 7.   Samuel Dana ordained Oct. 7, 1801.
Deacons in 1824
" John Goodwin chosen 1787 Nathan Bowen
" chosen 1788.

Here for the first time, we find the name of
John Avery in the list of the ministers of this
society. He had received a call to the office, but
never reached our shore, having been lost, with his
entire family, consisting of a wife and seven children, on their passage hither.

We can only account for the absence of both
record and tradition of the existence of this silver
memorial, by presuming that two members of the
committee wished to give to Mr. Reed the credit
that was due him, and believing that they would
'not be allowed so to do, with his knowledge, se-

14

cretly had the plate made, engraved and deposited where it was found. The secret was not revealed until May, 1886.

Mr. Reed's regard for the church was further shown by his will, confirmed by his widow Mrs. Hannah Reed, that gave to the church $11,000. The income of $7,000 to be used toward the pastor's salary, the income of $2,000 for the poor of church, the income of $1,000 for the Sunday-school, and $1,000 for a pastor's library, one half of which to be used for books to found the library and the income of the other half for annual additions to the same. The fund to be deposited with the Massachusetts Hospital Life Insurance Co.

The silver plate with various papers and records were placed in a copper box and rebuilt into the wall near the stone where it was found. The old pews were replaced with new, finished in the natural hard wood and cushioned, a new carpet was laid ; a new pulpit set was furnished, the organ was removed from the gallery to the orchestra at right of the pulpit, thoroughly overhauled and repaired ; a new bell weighing 1,557 lbs. was placed in the tower ; the roof re-shingled, and an iron fence placed upon the granite capping of the embankment wall in front of the entire premises.

All at a cost of $12,225.00.

Previous to 1890 the church had elected the superintendent of the Sunday-school as they had also elected the deacons, for life, or until they were dismissed. In that year it was voted to annually in the week next preceding the last Sunday in December elect the superintendent and assistant-superintendent of the Sunday-school for the term of one year.

In the year 1900 it was voted that the Board of Deacons shall consist of six persons, each elected for the term of six years. The time of the expiration of the term of office of those then serving was also fixed, as was the term of the three then elected, and that thereafter one be elected each year at the time of the election of the superintendent of the Sunday-school.

At a business meeting held in the chapel January 2, 1901, it was voted to publish a Church Manual containing the record of membership to the end of the nineteenth century and such other relative matter as the committee, having the compilation in charge shall consider desirable. It was also voted that the matter of a Church Manual be referred to the Church Committee with full authority to proceed to its publication and distribution.

Under authority given above the committee issue this Manual from August 13, 1684, to January 1, 1901.

The following " Confession of Faith and Covenant," were adopted at the organization of the church, August 13, 1684, and have remained in full force until the present time.

Confession of Faith.

ARTICLE 1.   We believe in one God, the Eternal Jehovah, infinite in wisdom, power, holiness, goodness and truth ;—the Foreordainer, Creator and Governor of all things ;—distinguished into three persons, the Father, the Son, and the Holy Ghost, having all of them the same Godhead, power and eternity.

ART. 2.   The Lord made man at first in his own image, in knowledge, righteousness and holiness ; from which state man falling by transgressing the law of his creation, all his posterity are corrupted in their whole nature,—averse to all good and strongly inclined to all evil, from whence do proceed all actual transgressions which bind men over to death, temporal, spiritual and eternal.

ART. 3.   God, out of his mere mercy, hath ordained his Son, the Lord Jesus, to be the Redeemer of man by the execution of his prophetical, priestly and kingly offices ; who, being truly God, took man's nature on him, yet without sin, being conceived by the power of the Holy Ghost, born of the virgin Mary, suffered, in that nature, the death of the cross to ransom the elect, was buried, and rose from the dead with the same body, with which he also ascended into heaven ; where, sitting at the right hand of God, he makes intercession for them

17

who believe on him, and from thence he shall return to judge the world at the last day.

ART. 4. In the new Covenant made by God with his people, the Holy Spirit of God works faith and repentance, and dwells in and with all such who are drawn truly to Christ; who, being united to him, are in this life pardoned and accounted righteous,—adopted,—in the whole man sanctified, —shall persevere to the end, and at last, in heaven, shall be actually glorified.

ART. 5. God hath given unto man the Scriptures of the Old and New Testament to be the only perfect, sufficient and perpetual rule of his faith and life,—not abolishing, but establishing the Law as a rule of righteousness for Christians to walk by, promising to accept of sincere obedience to the Law and Gospel through Christ,—when such as live and die unbelieving, impenitent and disobedient, shall suffer the vengeance of eternal fire.

ART. 6. All true believers make up that one body, the Church, of which Christ is head; who, for the gathering in and perfecting of his saints, hath appointed the Word, Prayer, Baptism and the Lord's Supper;—the Ministry, Officers and Discipline in particular Churches; and that, therefore, it is the duty of every Christian to attend carefully thereunto.

The following condensed Confession of Faith is used in receiving persons into the Communion of the Church.

ARTICLE 1. You believe in one living and true God, the Father, the Son and the Holy Ghost.

ART. 2. You believe that the Scriptures of the Old and New Testament were given by inspiration of God, and constitute an infallible rule of faith and practice.

ART. 3. You believe that by nature man is destitute of holiness and inclined to sin, so that without a change of heart he cannot enter the kingdom of God.

ART. 4. You believe that God, out of His love to man, gave His only begotten Son to be a sacrifice for sin ; and that by believing in Him we may be saved.

ART. 5. You believe in the resurrection of the dead, and in the day of judgment, when everyone shall give an account of himself to God, and the wicked shall go away into everlasting punishment, but the righteous into life eternal.

ART. 6. You believe that baptism and the Lord's Supper are the appointed sacraments of the Christian Church.

✠

The Covenant.

We do, in the presence of the Eternal God, under the sense of our great unworthiness personally to transact with so glorious a Majesty, acknowledge our inability to keep covenant with God, unless the Lord Jesus enables us thereunto by his Spirit,—with humble dependence on Him for gracious assistance, make and renew our Covenant with God and with one another as follows, viz :

ARTICLE 1. We do give up ourselves this day to the God whose name alone is Jehovah, Father, Son and Spirit, the only true and living God; and to our blessed Lord Jesus, as our only Redeemer and Saviour,—Prophet, Priest and King over our souls, and only Mediator of the Covenant of Grace; engaging our hearts to this God in Christ, by the help of his grace, to cleave unto him as one God and chief good, and unto Jesus Christ as one Mediator by faith, in a way of Gospel obedience, as becomes his covenant people forever,—engaging by the help of Christ to endeavor to keep ourselves pure, especially from the sins of the times, and to observe the Lord's commands in the exercise not only of public worship, but of private, in our families, by prayer and reading the Scriptures, and secret also, as God in His Word doth require.

ART. 2. We give up also our offspring unto God in Christ, avouching him to be our God and the God of our children; and ourselves with our children to be his people, humbly adoring his grace, that we and our children may be looked on as the Lord's, promising by his help (as far as there shall be need) to be instructing, catechizing, setting good patterns before them, and to be much in prayer for their conversion and salvation.

ART. 3. We do also give up ourselves one to another in the Lord, according to the will of God, to walk together as a particular Church of Christ, in all the ways of his worship and service, according to the rules of the Word of God ; promising in brotherly love faithfully to watch over one another's souls, and to submit ourselves to the discipline and government of Christ in this his church, and to the ministerial teaching, guidance and oversight of the elder or elders thereof and duly to attend the seals and censures and whatever ordinances Christ hath commanded to be observed by His people according to the order of the Gospel, in such degrees of communion unto which we have attained, so far as the Lord hath or shall reveal unto us ;—desiring also to walk with all regular and due communion with other churches, for the observing of which and all other covenant duties, we desire to depend wholly on the grace of God in Christ Jesus to enable us thereto, and wherein we shall fail, we shall humbly wait upon his grace in Christ for pardon, acceptance and healing for his name's sake. Amen.

The following abstract of the Covenant is used in receiving persons into the Communion of the Church.

Before the Lord, His holy angels and these witnesses, you acknowledge the Infinite Jehovah, Father, Son and Holy Spirit, as the only living and true God, and do solemnly avouch him to be your God and portion forever, giving yourself up to him in a perpetual covenant never to be forgotten ; to worship him in spirit and in truth, and to walk in all his commandments and ordinances blameless.

You give yourself to the Lord Jesus Christ, as God manifest in the flesh, the head of his believing people; and receive him as made of God unto you wisdom and righteousness and sanctification and redemption.

You give yourself to the Holy Spirit as your divine Enlightener, Guide and Comforter; desiring that all his work of grace may be effected in you; taking the Word of God, the Scriptures of the Old and New Testament, as your only rule of faith and practice.

Moreover, you give yourself to this Church in the Lord, promising, by divine help, in communion thereof, to attend upon the ordinances of the Gospel here administered, so long as your opportunity to be thus edified shall be continued to you; submitting yourself to the laws of Christ's kingdom duly administered, and to the watch and care of this Church in particular; promising that you will ever study to promote its peace, purity and prosperity.

Thus you covenant and engage; not depending on yourself, but on the mercy of him whose grace is sufficient for you.

(The Ordinance of Baptism is then Administered.)

In consequence of these professions and promises, we affectionately receive you as a member of this Church, and, in the name of Christ, declare you entitled to all its visible privileges.

And now, beloved in the Lord, let it be im-

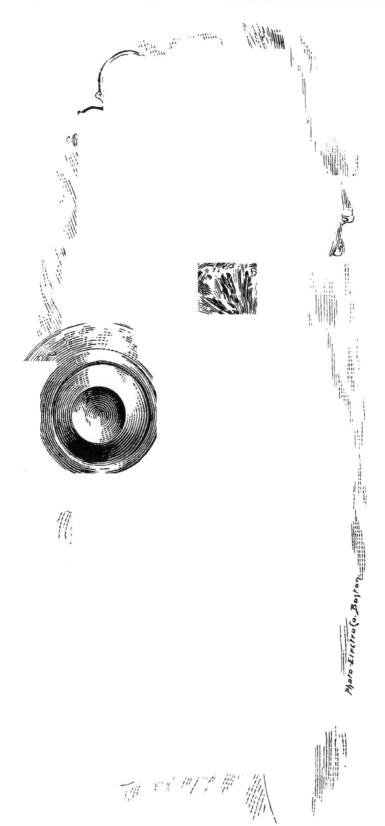

COMMUNION SERVICE.

Photo-Electro Co. Boston

pressed upon your mind that you have entered into solemn circumstances and engagements, from which you can never be released. Wherever you go, these vows will be upon you; they will follow you to the bar of God. Walk worthy, therefore, of your sacred profession. Be faithful unto death, and the Lord will give the crown of life.

We, on our part, promise, by divine assistance, to treat you with such affection and watchfulness as your new and tender relation to us demands. This we do, imploring to our common Lord that we and you may be steadfast in His covenant—may glorify Him with that holiness which becomes His professing people forever, and that hereafter, we may come, with all saints, in the unity of the faith and of the knowledge of the Son of God, "unto the measure of the stature of the fullness of Christ." Amen.

✠

Sacramental Service.

BY NATHAN P. SANBORN.

THE Sacramental Service of the Church consists of twenty-three pieces:

1 Baptismal Bowl,	12 Cups,
4 Flagons,	1 Plate,
4 Baskets,	1 Spoon.

The baskets, two of the cups and the spoon bear no inscription.

If the history of these vessels was written, there can be little doubt that with some of them it would begin with the organization of the Church. But there is neither written history nor tradition at present accessible that gives us any information in relation to them.

Three of the cups have the inscription M.C., and two others M.H.C., probably signifying Marblehead Church, and date back to a time when there was but one church in town.

Two others bear the inscription :

"BELONGING TO THE
FIRST CHURCH OF CHRIST IN-
MARBLEHEAD, 1728."

One other is inscribed,

"THE GIFT OF
WILL JONES AND RUTH WADLONS
TO THE FIRST CHURCH OF CHRIST
MARBLEHEAD,
A. D. 1730."

The record of October, 1730, tells us that "Mr. William Jones, dying, ordered his wife to give a small silver cup to ye Communion Table."

We also find that June 20, 1699, Moses Wadlon married Ruth Cheever, daughter of the pastor, who had united with the Church in 1692, and doubtless previous to 1730, gave a similar cup to the Church for the same purpose. And the record of December 21, 1772, explains why the two names appear on the same cup as follows : "Voted, that the two smallest vessels of the church plate be formed into one, and mark't w'h the names of the Donors."

The other two cups bear the inscription :
"THE LEGACY OF
GRACE THOMPSON
TO THE
FIRST CHURCH IN MARBLEHEAD,
1748.
REMODELED, in 1852."

In 1749 we find the record reads as follows :
"Capt. Tho's Gerry gave a silver Cann. w'g 15 oz.
15 pw., being a Legacy from Mrs. Grace Thompson
by Capt. Gerry, Executor."

The plate bears the following inscription :
"THE LEGACY OF
SAMUEL RUSSELL,
TO THE FIRST CHURCH IN MARBLEHEAD,
1723.
REMODELED, 1852."

We find on the record of 1725, " Mr. Samuel
Russell, who died May, 1725, gave a Legacy of 30
pounds to this church for the use of the communion table, which was made into a Silver
Tankard," and probably remained in that form until remodeled in 1852.

Each of the four flagons bears an inscription in
Latin. The first was given January 1, 1749, and
devoted to the Sacramental Service of this Church
by Rev. John Barnard, the second pastor. Inscription :

"Johannes Barnardus, Pastor Secundus primæ
Ecclesiæ Christi upud Marblehead, hanc Crateram

ad usum sacrosanctæ cænæ in Ecclesia dicta dedicavit.

"Jan. 1, 1748-9."

The next was on the same day, given by Robert
Hooper, Esq., and was also devoted to the Sacramental Service of the Church, as shown by the
following inscription :

" Robertus Huperus Arm. hanc crateram ad usum
sacrosanctæ cænæ in Ecclesia Christi prima Apud
Marblehead Dedicavit.

"Jan. 1, 1748-9."

The origin of the third fiagon is shown by the
following vote of the Church, May 7, 1759 :

" Voted to have a Flagon made out of the Legacy of Joseph Sweett, Esqr., with additions by his
heirs, Mr. Samuel Sweett, Mrs. Ruth Hooper, Mrs.
Martha Lee and Mr. Jos. Lemmon," which, with
the sacramental use for which it was set apart, is
stated in the following inscription :

" Hoc Legatum Josephi Sweett Ari. una cum Ad-
ditamenta ejus Hæredum Di S. Sweett, Dæ R.
Hooper, Dæ M. Lee et Di J. Lemmon ad usum
sacrosanctæ cænæ in prima Christi Ecclesia apud
Marblehead consecratum.   Maii 7, 1759."

The fourth flagon, as the inscription informs us,
was procured at the expense of the church
treasury, and devoted to the sacramental use of
this church. The treasury had no doubt been
replenished by the sale of such old plate as was
no longer required for use on account of the

recent donations, and also of the three Pewter Flagons given for the communion table in March, 1717, one by " Mrs. Sarah Dixey, wife of Dea. Dixey," one each by " Mr. Joshua Orne" and " J. B." (probably Rev. John Barnard who had then been settled not quite one year), from which, together with the accumulations from the ordinary collections, this flagon was purchased. The inscription is as follows :

" Hæc Lagena argentea ad usum sacrosanctæ cænæ in prima Christi Ecclesia apud Marblehead ex ejus Thesauro Consecrata, Maii 7, 1759."

The Baptismal Bowl has the following inscription :

" THE DONATION OF

DOC'R JOSEPH LEMMON,

TO THE FIRST CHURCH OF CHRIST IN

MARBLEHEAD,

A.D. 1773."

In the bottom is stamped the name of the manufacturer, " REVERE," undoubtedly the work of Paul Revere, who was at that time one of the principal silversmiths of Boston and who, a year and a half later, made himself famous by his patriotic ride to Lexington and Concord. There is also engraved upon it a beautiful picture of a swan plucking feathers from her breast to make a nest for her young.

Preachers and Pastors from 1638 to 1901.

WILLIAM WALTON, began preaching A.D., 1638. Died August or September, 1668. Service, 30 years.

REV. SAMUEL CHEEVER, began preaching October, 1668. Ordained, August 13, 1684. Died, May 29, 1724. Service, 55 years, 5 months.

REV. JOHN BARNARD, began preaching July 11, 1714. Ordained, July 18, 1716. Died, January 24, 1770. Service, 55 years.

REV. WILLIAM WHITWELL, ordained August 25, 1762. Died November 8, 1781. Service, 19 years.

REV. EBENEZER HUBBARD, ordained January 1, 1783. Died, October 15, 1800. Service, nearly 18 years.

REV. SAMUEL DANA, ordained October 7, 1801. Resigned, April 18, 1837. Service, 35 years, 6 months.

REV. SAMUEL COZZENS, ordained August 8, 1832. Resigned, April 18, 1837. Service, nearly 5 years.

Rev. Mark A. H. Niles, installed August 30, 1837. Resigned, November 27, 1844. Service, 7 years.

Rev. Edward A. Lawrence, installed April 23, 1845. Resigned, July 12, 1854. Service, 9 years.

Rev. Benjamin R. Allen, installed November 8, 1854. Died, June 2, 1872. Service, 18 years, 6 months.

Rev. John H. Williams, ordained September 3, 1873. Resigned, February 4, 1883. Service, 9 years, 5 months.

Rev. S. Linton Bell, installed February 28, 1884.

Deacons from 1684 to 1901.

Admitted.		Elected.		
1684	Gale, Benjamin,	1684		
1684	Reith, Richard,	1684		
1684	Stacey, John,	1703		
1701	Dixey, John,	1707		
1705	Skinner, Richard,	1707	dis.	1716
1703	White, John,	1716		
1726	Bayley, John,	1727	died	
1739	Hendley, Benjamin,	1749	"	
1739	Orne, Joshua, Jr.,	1749	"	
1743	Gale, William,	1759	"	
1736	Phillips, Stephen,	1765	"	
1754	Stacey, Benjamin,	1765	"	
1754	Williams, William,	1773	"	
1786	Goodwin, John,	1787	"	
1783	Bowen, Nathan,	1787	"	
1810	Homan, Richard,	1825	"	1851
1819	Phillips, Ichabod S.,	1825	dis.	1858
1816	Briggs, Calvin,	1851	died	1852
1834	Flint, David,	1852	"	1880
1843	Frost, Joseph,	1858	"	1882
1843	Rogers, Peter J.,	1859	"	1880
1850	Broughton, Glover, 2d,	1870	"	1887

1858	Pierce, Benjamin,	1870	dis. 1882
1874	Wormstead, William H.,	1879	" 1883
1877	Church, George R.,	1879	died 1900
1878	Knight, Benjamin F.,	1883	" 1886
1877	Grant, Richard T.,	1883	Term Expires 1901
1877	Broughton, Frank,	1886	" 1902
1877	Savory, Benjamin,	1886	" 1903
1877	Broughton, John G.,	1900	" 1904
1889	Tutt, Richard,	1900	" 1905
1885	Tutt, Edward D.,	1900	" 1906

☩

Sunday School Superintendents.

Rev. Samuel Dana, 1817 to 1818, self appointed.

Nathan Bowen, 1818 to 1820, appointed by Marblehead Sunday School Union.

Joseph Merrill, 1820 to 1821, appointed by Marblehead Sunday School Union.

Richard Homan, 1821 to 1829, appointed by Marblehead Sunday School Union.

Richard Homan, 1829 to 1851, elected by the church.

Ichabod S. Phillips, 1851 to 1856, elected by the church.

Nathan P. Sanborn, 1856 to 1890, elected by the church.

Benjamin Savory, 1890 to 1892, elected by the church.

John G. Broughton, February 10, 1892, elected by the church.

Assistant Superintendents.

Ichabod S. Phillips, 1845 to 1851, elected by the church.

Richardson Knowland, 1851 to 1854, elected by the church.

George R. Church, 1881 to 1890, elected by the church.

Walter M. Seavey, 1890 to 1891, elected by the church.

B. W. Tinker, February, 1892, to November, 1892, elected by the church.

Frank Broughton, December, 1892, elected by the church.

Alphabetical List of Members,

Explanation : Date in first column, year received.
(C) by confession. (L) by letter. (A) absent.
(Dis.) dismissed. ({) husband and wife.

1788		Abbott, Hannah,	Died	
1843		Aborn, Mary,	"	
1881	C	Adams, Mrs. Sarah,		
1892	C	Alden, Mrs. Lizzie A.,	Dis. March,	1895
1725		Allein, John,	Died	
1723		Allein, Mary,	"	
1839	C	Allen, Mrs. Elizabeth V.,	"	1894
1714		Allen, Elizabeth,		
1857	L	Allen, Mrs. Barbary M.,		
1857	L	Allen, Mrs. Martha B.,		
1858	L	Allen, Sarah 'A.,	"	1883
1858	L	Allen, Sophia E.,	"	1883
1685		Allen, Robella,	"	
1685		Allin, John,	Dis,	
1834	C	Andrews, Augustus,	"	
1832	C	Andrews, Mary L.,	Died	
1697		Andrews, Mary,	"	
1838	C	Anthony, Mrs. Hannah,	"	1888

1861	C Anthony, Rebecca F.,	Died	1866
1839	C Anthony, William C.,	"	
1819	C Appleton, Alice,		
1850	C Appleton, Daniel,		
1825	Appleton, Mary,	Died	
1825	Appleton, Sarah,	"	
1827	Appleton, Sarah F.,		
1834	C Appleton, Thomas	"	1855
1684	Ashwood, Elizabeth,		
1786	Ashton, Anna,		
1729	Ashton, Margaret,		
1728	Ashton, Mary, Sen.,		
1714	Ashton, Philip,		
1743	Ashton, Sarah,		
1810	Ashton, Sarah,		
1832	Ashton, Sarah,		
1843	C Atkins, Ambrose H.,		
1894	C Atkins, Hannah,		
1843	Atkins, Hannah P.,	Died	
1893	C Atkins, Nathaniel H.,		
1874	C Atkins, Rebecca P.,		
1818	Atkins, Sarah,	Died	
1833	Avery, Amanda,	"	
1829	Avery, Cynthia		
1847	Avery, Frances,		
1833	Avery, Frances,		
1833	Avery, Mary,		
1824	Avery, Mary Ann,		
1824	Avery, Samuel,		
1833	Avery, Sophia,		

34

1763		Bacon, Hannah,	Died	
1763		Bacon, Sarah,	"	
1862	C	Bailey, Annie,	"	1868
1766		Bailey, Elizabeth,		
1824		Bailey, Mary,		
1876	C	Bailey, Mary B.,		
1774		Barber, Martha,	Died	
1811		Barber, Miriam,	"	
1820		Barker, Eliza,		
1727		Barker, Ruth,		
1719		Barnard, Anna,		
1828		Barnes, Ann P.,		
1684		Barrett, Ann,	"	
1890	L	⎰ Barr, John,	Dis.	1899
1890	L	⎱ Barr, Elizabeth,	"	1899
1877	L	Barry, Mrs. Dora, (Tindley)		
1838	C	Bartlett, Abigail H.	Died	
1888	C	Bartlett, Mrs. Cora L., (Tucker)		
1768		Bartlett, Elizabeth,	Died	
1819		Bartlett, John, 4th,	"	
1695		Bartlett, Mary,		
1770		Bartlett, Mary,		
1824		Bartlett, Mary,		
1830		Bartlett, Mary,		
1703		Bartlett, Rebecca,	"	
1829		Bartlett, Rebecca,	Dis.	
1824		Bartlett, Ruth,	Died	
1708		Bartlett, Sarah,	"	
1866	C	Bartol, Annie,	Dis.	
1871	C	Bartol, Emma, (Clemons)		

35

1843	C	Bartol, John,	Died	
1832	C	Bartol, John, Jr.,	Dis.	
1818		Bartol, Rebecca,	Died	
1832	C	{ Bartol, William T.	"	
1847	C	{ Bartol, Sarah L.,	"	1892
1684		**Bartoll, Mary,**		
1684		**Bartoll, William,**		
1818		Bassett, Elizabeth,	"	
1871	C	Bassett, Mrs. Margaret,	Dis.	1885
1834		Bassett, Samuel P.,	Died	
1705		**Batchelour, Sarah,**	"	
1711		**Batchelour, William,**		
1858	C	Bateman, Peter,	"	1858
1876	C	Bates, Maria L.,		
1803		Batt, Elizabeth,	Died	
1823		{ Battys, Jonas,	"	
1823		{ Battys, Sally,		
1726		Bayley, John		
1689		Beale, Martha,		
1719		Beale, Sarah,		
1684		Beal, William,		
1698		Beal, William,		
1687		Bell, Jane,		
1884	L	{ BELL, REV. S. LINTON,		
1889	C	{ Bell, Mrs. Leila E.,	.	
1788		Bennett, Elizabeth,	Died	
1705		Bennett, Susanna,	"	
1819		Berry, Betsey,		
1832		Bessom, Elizabeth,		
1876	C	Bessom, Mrs. Ellen,		

1825	Bessom, John,	Died	
1838	Bessom, Miriam R.,	Dis.	
1825	Bessom, Rebecca,	Died	
1834	Bessom, Sarah,	"	1883
1877 L	Bird, Mrs. Nancy,	Dis.	1890
1738	Birk, Deliverance,	Died	
1732	Bishop, Eleanor,	"	
1699	Blackington, Pentecost,		
1719	Blackington, Pentecost,		
1719	Blackington, Rebecca,		
1714	Blackler, Elizabeth,		
1803	Blackler, Elizabeth,		
1830	Blackler, Emily,	"	
1838	Blackler, Hannah H.,	Dis.	
1684	Blackler, Jane,	Died	
1830	Blackler, Lucia,	"	
1830	Blackler, Lucy Ann,	"	
1850	Blackler, Lydia H.,	Dis.	
1858 C	Blackler, Mrs. Mary E.		
1843	Blackler, Mary Reed,	Died	
1848	Blackler, Martha H.,	"	
1806	Blackler, Nancy,		
1828	Blackley, Mary,	"	
1829	Blanchard, Ann,	Ex.	
1838	Blanchard, Sarah B.,	Died	
1834	Blaney, Elizabeth,	"	1856
1850 C	Blaney, Rebecca B.,	Died Aug. 12, 1899	
1871 C	Boardman, Mrs. Susan G.,		
1830	Boden, Hannah,	Died	
1823	Boden, Nancy,	"	

1838		Boden, Ruth, Sen.,	Died
1838		Boden, Ruth,	"
1820		Boden, Sarah,	"
1830		Bond, Margaret,	Dis.
1684		Bondfield, George,	Died
1750		Bowden, Elizabeth,	"
1810		Bowden, Elizabeth,	
1727		Bowden, Francis,	
1834		Bowden, John,	
1843		Bowden, John D.,	
1716		Bowden, Mary,	
1821		Bowden, Mary,	
1839		Bowden, Mary H.,	
1738		Bowden, Michael,	
1850		Bowden, Ruth,	
1762		Bowden, Sarah,	
1784		Bowden, Sarah,	
1820		Bowden, Sarah C.,	
1784		Bowen, Elizabeth,	
1805		Bowen, Elizabeth,	
1783		Bowen, Deacon Nathan,	
1877	L	{ Bowman, William W.,	
1877	L	{ Bowman, Mrs. Sarah A.,	
1695		Boobyer, Joan,	
1707		Boobyer, Margaret,	"
1853	C	Bradbury, Mrs. Eliza B., (Hooper)	
1800		Bradeen, Mercy,	Died
1898	C	Bragdon, Mrs. Mary Eliza,	
1695		Brattle, Mary,	Died
1810		Brawden, Margaret,	"

1739		Bray, Alice,	Died
1832		Bray, Evelina,	"
1819		Bray, Hannah H.,	
1824		Bray, Isabella,	
1760		Bray, Jean,	"
1830	C	Bray, Mrs. Nancy,	Died, April 29, 1877
1803		Bray, Sarah,	Died
1888	C	Breare, Mrs. Abbie, (Martin)	
1731		Breed, Ruth,	Died
1687		Brentnall, Sarah,	"
1892	C	Brewer, John M.,	
1871	C	Brewer, Mrs. Sarah L.,	
1845	C	Bridgeo, Clarissa,	Died March 2, 1881
1838		Bridgeo, Clarissa,	Died
1818		Bridgeo, Deliverance,	"
1825		Bridgeo, Hannah,	
1834		Bridgeo, Harriet,	
1819		Bridgeo, Jane,	
1794		Bridgeo, Mary,	
1787		Bridgeo, Mary,	
1825		Bridgeo, Mary,	"
1829	C	Bridgeo, Mrs. Mary,	Died April 24, 1887
1845		Bridgeo, Nancy,	Died
1834		Bridgeo, Nancy,	" 1855
1689		Briers, Elizabeth,	
1833		Briggs, Ann W.,	
1816		Briggs, Calvin,	
1816		Briggs, Rebecca,	"
1841		Briggs, Caroline,	Dis.
1834		Briggs, Clarissa,	Died

1843		Briggs, Elizabeth,	Died	
1838		Briggs, Harriet,	"	
1838		Briggs, Mary S.,		
1850		Briggs, Rebecca W.,		
1785		Brimblecomb, Alice,		
1739		Brimblecomb, Deborah,		
1716		Brimblecomb, Elizabeth,		
1803		Brimblecomb, Eleanor,		
1810		Brimblecomb, Elizabeth,		
1739		Brimblecomb, Hannah,		
1784		Brimblecomb, Hannah,		
1742		Brimblecomb, Joseph,		
1768		Brimblecomb, Miriam,		
1711		Brimblecomb, Sarah,		
1832		Broughton, Elizabeth,	"	
1850		Broughton, Elizabeth S.,	Dis.	
1874	C	Broughton, Emma,	"	1895
1861		Broughton, Emma S.,		
1877	C	Broughton, Deacon Frank,		
1831		⎰ Broughton, Glover,	Died	
1832	C	⎱ Broughton, Mrs. Elizabeth H.,	"	1891
1850	C	Broughton, Deacon Glover,	"	1887
1877	C	⎰ Broughton, Deacon John G.,		
1868	C	⎱ Broughton, Mrs. Mary L., (Chamberlin)		
1884	C	Broughton, Mary S.,		
1825		Broughton, Nancy,	Died	
1825		Broughton, Nicholson,	"	
1843		Broughton, N. H.,		
1741		Broughton, Sarah,		
1771		Broughton, Sarah,		

1843		Broughton, Susan G.,	Dis.	
1884	C	Broughton, William H.,	"	1885
1793		Brown, Anna,	Died	
1807		Brown, Annie,	"	
1834		Brown, Benjamin B.,	"	
1825	C	Brown, Mrs. Elizabeth, Died Feb. 18, 1881		
1891	C	Brown, Frank F.,		
1819		Brown, Hannah,	Died	
1783		Brown, Jane,	"	
1819		Brown, John,		
1877	C	Brown, Mrs. Lizzie S.,		
1784		Brown, Mary,	Died	
1755		Brown, Mary,	"	
1825		Brown, Mary,		
1830		Brown, Mary,		
1831		Brown, Mary,		
1877	L	Brown, Mrs. Mary E.,		
1832		Brown, Peter,	Died	
1834		Brown, Ruth Ann,	"	
1843		Brown, Rebecca,		
1755		Brown, Sarah,		
1759		Brown, Sarah,		
1821		Brown, Sarah,		
1843		Brown, Sarah,		
1878	L	Brown, Mrs. Sarah H.,		
1834		Brown, William P.,	Died 1883	
1843		Brown, William P.,	"	
1688		Browne, Elizabeth,	Dis.	
1832		Bubier, Eliza,	Died	
1847	L	Bubier, Eliza,	Dis.	

1767	Bubier, Ruth,	Died	
1684	Buckley, Sarah,	"	
1742	Bull, Sarah,		
1800	Burnham, Mary,		
1725	Burroughs, Mary,	"	
1884	Burroughs, Mrs. Annie, (Gregory)		
1763	Bussey, Mary,	Died	
1738	Cain, Judith,	Died	
1810	Calley, Elizabeth,	"	
1727	Calley, Francis,		
1805	Candler, Abagail,		
1832	Candler, Hannah,		
1703	Cannon, Sarah,		
1702	Carder, Elizabeth,		
1708	Carder, John, Sen.,		
1684	Carder, Rebecca,		
1877 L	Carleton, Mrs. Hannah H.,		
1892 C	Carr, Walter,		
1832	Carroll, Jane,	Died	
1791	Cash, Hannah,	"	
1834	Cass, Arabella,		
1834 .	Cass, Jonathan,	"	1859
1886 C	Caswell, Mrs. Elizabeth J.,	"	1897
1825 C	Caswell, Mrs. Jane, 95 years,	"	1882
1888 C	⌠ Caswell, John C.,	"	1897
1877 L	⌡ Caswell, Mrs. Mary,	"	1894
1829	Caswell, Nancy,		
1728	Candish, Susanna,		
1706	Cauley, Martha,		

1717	Cavendish, Sarah,	Died	
1880 L	⎰ Chadwick, Benjamin W.,		
1880 L	⎱ Chadwick, Mrs. Stella,		
1832	Chadwick, Joanna,	Dis.	
1830	Chambers, Ephraim,	Died	
1858 C	⎰ Chamberlin, George, Died Nov. 8,		1884
1856 C	⎱ Chamberlin, Mrs. Mary E., Died		1897
1825	Chambers, Hannah,	"	
1877 L	Chambers, Mrs. Harriet B.,	"	1884
1718	Chapman, Dorcas,		
1762	Chapman, Eliza,		
1887 C	Chapman, Mrs. Harriet B.		
1829 C	Chapman, Mrs. Leonora,	Died	1877
1729	Charder, Elizabeth,	"	
1726	Chardee, Rebekah,		
1898 L	Chase, Mrs. Rebecca E.,		
1707	Cheever, Amos,	Died	
1702	Cheever, Mary,	"	
1684	⎰ CHEEVER, REV. SAMUEL,	"	1724
1684	⎱ Cheever, Mrs. Ruth,		
1692	Cheever, Ruth,		
1702	Cheever, Sarah,		
1706	Cheever, Mr. Thomas,		
1737	Chewt, Abigail,		
1733	Chewt, James, Jr.,		
1789	Chin, Elizabeth,		
1742	Chin, John,		
1703	Chin, Rebecca,		
1742	Chin, Rebeckah,		
1834	Chinn, John,	"	1855

1877 L Chinn, Mrs. Eliza P.,

1877 L Chinn, Emma H.,   Dis. Dec., 1889

1824   Chinn, Sally,   Died

1843   Chinn, Samuel,   "   1869

1834   Chinn, Robert,

1888 C Chisholm, Mrs. Jane E.,

1739   Chub, Mary,   Died

1877 L ⎰ Church, Deacon George R.,   "   1900

1877 L ⎱ Church, Mrs. Hannah H.,

1877 L Church, Mrs. Mary,   Died

1894 C ⎰ Church, William R.,

1887 L ⎱ Church, Mrs. Annie M.,(Lind)

1718   Chute, Mary,   Died

1722   Chute, Thomas,   "

1684   Clark, Abagail,

1756   Clark, Mary,   "

1877 L Clark, Mrs. Mary A.,   Died Jan. 28, 1887

1876 C Clark, Mrs. Sarah, (Tucker)   Died 1900

1684   Clattery, Mary,   "

1858 C ⎰ Clothey, John, 2d,   "   1893

1850 C ⎱ Clothey, Mrs. Elizabeth J.,   "   1882

1868 C Clothey, Joseph,

1885 C Clough, Mrs. Ella F., (Dinsmore)

1820   Clough, Lydia,   Died

1825 C Cloutman, Mrs. Almira,   "   1890

1814   Cloutman, Anna,

1829   Cloutman, Ellen,

1834   Cloutman, Eleanor,   "

1825   Cloutman, Hannah,   Dis.

1877 L Cloutman, Hannah, Died Sept. 14, 1884

1876	C	Cloutman, Mrs. Harriet G.,	Died	1884
1834		Cloutman, Henry,	"	1850
1850		Cloutman, H. B.,	Dis.	
1881	C	Cloutman, Lizzie K.,	Died	1896
1728		Cloutman, Mary,	"	
1829		Cloutman, Mary,		
1812		Cloutman, Nancy,		
1834		Cloutman, Nancy E.,		
1834		Cloutman, Rebecca T.,		
1819		Cloutman, Susannah,	"	
1850		Cloutman, S. Eliz.,	Dis.	
1706		Cooke, Hannah,	Died	
1684		Coas, Grace,	"	
1718		Coas, Rachael,		
1718		Coats, Mary,	"	
1898	C	Coates, Nellie A.,	Dis.	1898
1685		Codner, Rachel,	Died	
1766		Codner, Sarah,	"	
1771		Coes, Thomas,		
1829		Cogswell, Francis,		
1892	C	Cole, Mrs. Rebecca, (Usher)		
1763		Cole, Ruth,	Died	
1760		Collins, Hannah, Jr.,	"	
1763		Collins, Mary,		
1700		Collins, Naomi,		
1877	L	Collyer, Mrs. Catherine,		
1741		Collyer, Eliza,	Died	
1684		Conant, Elizabeth,	"	
1887	L	Connelly, Jane, (McLean) Dis. Jan. 1888		
1894	C	Conway, Ada R.,		

1887	C	Conway, Florence G.		
1861	C	⎰ Conway, John,	Died Jan. 20,	1880
1861	C	⎱ Conway, Hannah,	Died	1867
1876	C	⎰ Conway, John, Jr.;	"	1896
1876	L	⎱ Conway, Mrs. Amanda P.,		
1721		Cook, Anna,	Died	
1722		Cook, Augustine,	"	
1829		Coombs, Hannah,		
1895	L	Corner, John,		
1781		Cornal, Elias,	Died	
1702		Cotton, Mr. Josiah,	"	
1843	C	⎰ Courtis, William,	Died Nov. 7,	1878
1843		⎱ Courtis, Mahitable A.,	Died	1864
1874	C	Courtis, Mrs. Carrie A., (Frost)		
1850		Cowell, Abagail,	Died	
1746		Cowell, Jemimah,	"	
1850		Creecy, M. Caroline,	Ex.	
1853		Creesy, Joanna P.,	"	
1830		Creesy, Josiah P.,	Died	
1830		Creesy, Mary,	Ex.	
1833		Creesy, Mary,	"	
1833		Creesy, Sarah H.,	"	
1877	L	Cressy, Mrs. Mary B.,	Died	1877
1818		Cross, Abagail,	"	
1876	C	⎰ Cross, Albert L.,	Dis.	1883
1881	C	⎱ Cross, Mrs. Carrie,(Broughton)	"	1886
1876	C	Cross, Annie R.,	"	1883
1871	C	Cross, Hannah R.,		
1855	L	Cross, Maria L.,	Dis.	
1838	C	Cross, Mrs. Mary,	Died Oct. 1,	1885

1849	C	Cross, Mary A.,	
1829		Crowninshield, Mary,	Dis.
1817		Crowninshield, Sarah,	Died
1817		Crowninshield, William,	"
1701		Cruf, Elenor,	"
1852		{ Currier, G. W.,	Dis. 1854
1852		{ Currier, Laura A.,	" 1854
1742		Curtis, Margaret,	Died
1739		Curtis, Ruth,	"
1858	C	Cushing, Mrs. Elizabeth,	" 1883
1685		Dallabar, Joseph, Sen.,	Died
1685		Dallabar, Margaret,	"
1684		Dallabar, Mary,	Dis.
1706		Damon, Rebecca,	Died
1839		Dana, Abagail F.,	"
1850	C	Dana, Anna H.,	" 1892
1830		Dana, Henrietta B.,	
1834		Dana, Mary D.,	
1801		{ DANA, REV. SAMUEL,	
1808		{ Dana, Henrietta,	
1839	C	Dana, Sarah E.,	" 1891
1684		Darby, Alice,	
1764		Darling, Eleanor,	
1725		Darling, James,	
1717		Darling, Joanna,	
1725		Darling, Joanna,	
1770		Darrel, Sarah,	
1770		Darrel, Thos. Phipps,	
1810		Davis, Mary,	

1819	Davis, Thomas,	Died	
1847	Davis, Thomas A.,	"	1850
1847	Davis, Rebecca,		
1868 C	{ Day, Benjamin,		
1850 C	{ Day, Mrs. Hannah V.,	Died 1882	
1878 C	{ Day, Benjamin F.,		
1878 C	{ Day, Mrs. Harriet,	Died 1886	
1876 C	Day, Emma,	Dis. Feb. 16, 1890	
1877 C	Day, Mrs. Mary, (Hill)		
1817	Deacons, Deborah,	Died	
1734	Dean, Eliza,	"	
1884 C	Denning, Mrs. Wilhelmina A.,		
1746	Dennis, Amos,	Died	
1827	Dennis, Ann,	"	
1738	Dennis, Anna,		
1834	Dennis, Archibald S.,	"	1859
1870	{ Dennis, Daniel,	Dis.	
1870	{ Dennis, Mary,	"	
1850	Dennis, Deliverance K.,	"	
1774	Dennis, Elizabeth,	Died	
1810	Dennis, Elizabeth,	"	
1830	Dennis, Elizabeth,		
1717	Dennis, James,		
1738	Dennis, Johannah,		
1794	Dennis, John,		
1825	Dennis, Jonas,		
1810	Dennis, Lois,		
1794	Dennis, Lydia,		
1760	Dennis, Mary,		
1819	Dennis, Rebecca,		

1774	Dennis, Rebekah,	Died
1688	Dennis, Sarah,	"
1724	Dennis, Sarah,	
1750	Dennis, Sarah,	
1765	Dennis, Sarah,	
1796	Dennis, Sarah,	
1805	Dennis, Sarah,	
1713	Dennis, Susanna,	
1824	Devereux, Alice B.,	
1762	Devereux, Anna,	
1739	Devereux, Elizabeth,	"
1877 L	Devereux, Elizabeth,	Died June, 1887
1828	Devereux, Elizabeth B.,	Died
1828	Devereux, Elizabeth G.,	"
1727	Devereux, Hannah,	
1758	Devereux, Hannah,	
1837	Devereux, Hannah,	
1735	Devereux, Humphrey,	
1759	Devereux, Humphrey,	
1774	Devereux, Lois,	
1789	Devereux, Mary,	
1825	Devereux, Mary,	"
1843	Devereux, Mary B.,	Ex.
1754	Devereux, Ralph,	Died
1839	Devereux, Ralph,	"
1739	Devereux, Robert,	
1800	Devereux, Robert,	
1738	Devereux, Ruth,	
1822	Devereux, Sally P.,	
1690	Devereux, Susannah,	

1804		Devereux, Tabitha,	Died
1753		Diamond, Eunice,	"
1819		Dike, Elizabeth,	
1715		Dimond, Johannah,	
1874	C	Dinsmore, Hattie,	
1762		Dixey, Agnes,	Died
1716		Dixey, Ann,	"
1830		Dixey, Eliza,	"
1843	C	Dixey, Mrs. Eliza,	Died May, 1881
1843		Dixey, Hannah,	Died
1834		Dixey, Hannah G.,	" 1874
1766		Dixey, Jane,	
1701		Dixey, John,	
1716		Dixey, Margaret,	
1894	C	Dixey, Martha Ellen,	
1684		Dixey, Mary,	Died
1804		Dixey, Mary,	"
1796		Dixey, Rebecca,	
1830		Dixey, Rebecca,	
1843		{ Dixey, Richard W.,	" 1860
1842	C	{ Dixey, Rebecca B.,	" 1896
1759		Dixey, Tabitha,	..
1879	C	Dixie, Benjamin,	Died Nov. 11, 1884
1810		Doak, Deliverance,	Died
1834		Doak, Elizabeth,	"
1803		Doak, Mary,	
1834		Doak, Mary,	
1819		Doak, Michael,	
1800		Doak, Sarah,	
1724		Doake, Elizabeth,	

50

1728		Dod, Abagail,		Died	
1728		Dod, Elizabeth,		"	
1728		Dod, Hannah,			
1737		Dod, Mary,			
1725		Dod, Priscilla,			
1684		Dod, Sarah,			
1728		Dod, Sarah,			
1700		Dodd, Thomas, Sen.,			
1701		Dodd, Mary, Jr.,			
1696		Dodd, Mary,			
1763		Dodd, Susannah,		"	
1889	C	Dodge, Mrs. Mary S.,		Died	1894
1825		Doliber, Eliza,		"	
1843		Doliber, Elizabeth,		"	1867
1858	C	Doliber, Elizabeth D.,		"	1900
1723		Doliber, Annice,			
1877	L	Doliber, Mrs. Isabella,			
1766		Doliber, Jane,		Died	
1829		Doliber, John,		"	
1840		Doliber, Joseph,	Died Aug. 20,	1868	
1702		Doliber, Mary,		Died	
1726		Doliber, Mary,		"	
1808		Doliber, Mary,			
1818		Doliber, Mary,			
1800		Doliber, Peter,			
1829		Doliber, Sarah,			
1832		Doliber, Sarah,			
1834		Doliber, Sarah,		"	1853
1716		Doliver, Mary,			
1810		Doliver, Sarah Orne,			

1755	Dolliber, Hannah,	Died	
1748	Dolliver, Elizabeth,	"	
1753	Dolliver, Elizabeth,		
1729	Dolliver, Samuel, Jr.,		
1757	Duggens, Hannah,		
1758	Duggens, Mary,		
1728	Dyer, Anna,		

1893	C ⌠ Eastland, Thomas S.,		
1893	C ⌡ Eastland, Mrs. Esther E.,		
1772	Eaton, Benjamin,	Died	
1853	C Eaton, Mrs. Bridget,	Died Nov. 1885	
1761	Eaton, Mary,	Died	
1885	C Eaton, Mary E.,	Died Dec. 8, 1894	
1830	Eaton, Nancy,	Died	
1714	Edgecomb, Grace,	Dis.	
1714	Edgecomb, Mary,	Died	
1748	Edgecomb, Miriam,	"	
1695	Edgecomb, Rachel,		
1727	Edden, Jean,	"	
1886	L ⌠ Eddy, William,	Died Feb. 21, 1889	
1886	L ⌡ Eddy, Mrs. Ella J.,	Dis. 1891	
1704	Elcoat, Esther,	Died	
1688	Eliot, Elizabeth,	"	
1743	Eletrope, Hannah,		
1723	Eletrope, Martha,		
1716	Elethrop, Mary		
1684	Ellis, Margaret,		
1723	Elkins, Elizabeth,		
1818	Elkins, Mary,		

1845		Elkins, Mary,	Died 1862
1802		Elkins, Thomas, Jr.,	"
1800		Elkins, Rebecca,	
1898	C	Eustis, Charles L.,	
1897	C	{ Eustis, Clarence F.,	
1890	L	{ Eustis, Mrs. Clarence F.,	
1851		Evans, Evan,	Dis.
1879	C	Evans, Ellen,	" 1883
1725		Evans, Mary,	Died
1729		Evans, Nathaniel,	"
1877	L	Evans, William T.,	
1882	L	Eveleth, Philemon,	Died May 14, 1900
1689		Fabiaus, Joanna,	Died
1719		Fabius, Joannah,	"
1830		Felton, Elizabeth,	
1743		Felton, John,	
1718		Felton, Mary,	
1888	C	Felton, Mrs. Mary E.,	
1728		Felton, Sarah,	Died
1816		Felt, Thomas,	"
1717		Ferguson, Archibald,	
1867	C	{ Ferguson, Augustus P.,	
1857	C	{ Ferguson, Mrs. Caroline E.,	
1888	C	Ferguson, Emily G.,	Died Aug. 4, 1892
1684		Ferguson, Mary,	Died
1781		Feteplace, Elizabeth,	"
1772		Feteplace, Rebecca,	
1796		Fettyplace, Edward,	
1783		Fettyplace, Jane,	

1836	C	Fettyplace, Lucy C. D., Died Jan. 4, 1886
1796		Fettyplace, Sarah, Died
1834		Fielding, Abagail, " 1880
1851		Fielding, Ruth A.,
1716		Fife, Eliza,
1711		Finch, Hannah,
1690		Finch, Rebecca,
1731		Flack, Mary,
1727		Flack, Samuel, "
1834	C	{ Flint, Deacon David, Died May 9, 1880
1834	C	{ Flint, Mrs. Ruth H., Died Mar. 13, 1889
1795		Flint, Elizabeth, Died
1878	C	Flint, Lizzie R., Died Jan. 29, 1896
1825		Flint, Ruth, Died
1858		Flint, Ruth H., Dis. R. I.
1875	C	Florence, Mrs. Emma R.,
1898	L	Ford, Lizzie,
1831		{ Foss, Thomas, Died Feb. 9, 1883
1877	L	{ Foss, Mrs. Eliza C., " July 20, 1887
1877	L	Foss, Ida C.,
1897	C	Foss, Jennie P.,
1684		Fortune, Mary, Died
1707		Fortune, Sarah, "
1756		Foster, Ebenezer,
1760		Foster, Elizabeth,
1771		Foster, Sarah,
1752		Fowls, Jacob,
1800		Fowler, Sarah,
1829		Francis, Frances,
1850	C	Franks, Mrs. Sarah G.,

1876	C	Frederick, Emily,	Died Nov. 21, 1883
1876	C	Frederick, Martha,	
1829		Freeto, Elizabeth,	Died
1877	C	⎰ Freeto, Frank,	
1877	C	⎱ Freeto, Mrs. Frances A. (Haskell)	
1885	C	Freeto, Fred B.,	
1818		Freeto, Grace,	Died
1843		⎰ Freeto, John,	"
1825		⎱ Freeto, Mrs. Mary, Died June 25, 1889	
1834		Freeto, Mary E.,	Dis.
1850	C	Freeto, Mrs. Mahitable J.,	
1876	C	Freeto, Philip,	
1810		Freeto, Sarah,	Died
1755		Freetoo, Hannah, ·	"
1742		Freetow, Mary,	
1900	C	Frost, Abbie Francis,	
1843	C	⎧ Frost, Dea. Joseph, Died Jan. 15, 1882	
1832		⎨ Frost, Remember,	Died
1865	C	⎩ Frost, Mrs. Mary G., Died Mar. 26, 1893	
1827		Frost, Rachel,	Died
1732		Funel, Prudence,	"
1710		Furnace, David,	
1783		Furniss, Sarah,	
1894	C	Gage, Mrs. Jennie H., (Stacey)	
1729		Gale, Abagail,	Died
1684		Gale, Ambrose,	"
1715		Gale, Ambrose,	"
1694		Gale, Ambrose, Jr.,	"
1684		Gale, Benjamin,	"

1695		Gale, Deborah,	Died
1684		Gale, Deliverance,	"
1723		Gale, Eleanor,	
1753		Gale, Elizabeth,	
1807		Gale, Elizabeth,	
1734		Gale, Hannah,	
1686		Gale, Mary,	
1728		Gale, Mary,	
1751		Gale, Mary,	
1728		Gale, Samuel,	
1695		Gale, Sarah,	
1740		Gale, Sarah,	
1733		Gale, Susannah,	
1743		Gale, William,	
1895	L	Gallagher, Joseph W.,	
1740		Gallison, Agnes,	Died
1706		Gallison, Jane,	Dis.
1854		Gammell, Har't M.,	Died
1834		Gardner, Abel,	Dis.
1825		Gardner, Elizabeth,	Died
1825		Gardner, Jane,	"
1850		Gardner, Mary B.,	"
1874	C	Gardner, Mrs. Susie M., (Snow)	
1825		Garney, Hannah,	Died
1871	C	Garney, John G. C.,	
1783		Garney, Margaret,	Died
1836		Garney, Margaret,	"
1818		Garney, Mary,	
1832		Garney, Susanna,	
1840		Garney, Thomas,	

1789		Gatchel, Eunice,	Died
1684		Gatchell, Elizabeth,	"
1737		Gerry, Elizabeth, ·	
1737		Gerry, Thomas,	
1897	C	Getchell, Mrs. Mary A.,	
1728		Giffard, Rebekah,	Died
1728		Giffard, Robert, Jr.,	"
1763		Giffard, Sarah,	"
1695		Gifford, Mary,	Dis.
1695		Gifford, Robert,	Died
1718		Gilbert, Daniel,	"
1720		Gilbert, Elizabeth,	
1850		{ Gile, Daniel,	" 1872
1852	L	{ Gile, Mrs. Susan J. D.,	
1876	C	Gile, Mrs. Deliverance (Lindsey) Dis. 1885	
1879	C	{ Gill, Asa W.,	Died May 19, 1889
1879	C	{ Gill, Mrs. Asa W.,	Died 1890
1842		Gilley, John,	Dis.
1842	·	Gilley, Mary,	Died
1818		Gillie, Sally,	"
1895	C	Gillis, Mrs. Christie,	
1789		Girdler, Anna,	Died
1720		Girdler, Benjamin,	"
1842		Girdler, Eliza,	
1723		Girdler, Elizabeth,	
1830		Girdler, Elizabeth,	
1684		Girdler, Francis, .	
1832		Girdler, Grace,	
1858	C	Girdler, Mrs. Grace,	
1888	C	Girdler, Lizzie V.,	" 1893

1808		Girdler, Margaret,	Died	
1750		Girdler, Mary,	"	
1858	C	Girdler, Mrs. Mary A.,	"	1878
1880	C	Girdler, Mrs. Mary E.,	"	1899
1871	C	Girdler, Mary L.,		
1808		Girdler, Rebecca,	Died	
1723		Girdler, Robert,	"	
1704		Girdler, Sarah,		
1684		Glass, Elizabeth,		
1871	C	Glass, Mrs. Mary,		
1757		Glover, Abagail,	Died	
1784		Glover, Hannah,	"	
1783		Glover, Jonathan, Esq.,		
1787		Glover, Mary,		
1724		Gold, Mary, .	"	
1886	C	Goldthwait, Joel E.,	Dis.	1894
1877	L	Goldthwait, Mrs. Mary L.,		
1787		Gondy, Elizabeth,	Died	
1748		Goodwin, Hepsibah,	"	
1843	C	Goodwin, Hannah,	"	1900
1748		Goodwin, Jean, Jr.,		
1786		Goodwin, John,		
1834		Goodwin, John,	"	1858
1807		Goodwin, Joseph,		
1788		Goodwin, Mary,		
1788		Goodwin, Mary,		
1843	C	Goodwin, Mary Jane,	"	1900
1803		Goodwin, Nancy,		
1810		Goodwin, Rebecca T.,		
1850	C	Goodwin, Rebecca T.,		

1826		Goodwin, Sally,	.	Died	
1721		Goodwin, Samuel,		"	
1707		Goodwin, Sarah,			
1787		Goodwin, Sarah,			
1834		Goodwin, Susannah,			
1866	C	Goodwin, Mrs. Tabitha,		"	1896
1807		Goodwin, William,			
1756		Goodwin, William, Jr.,		"	
1884	C	Goss, Mary R.,	Died June 28, 1886		
1876	C	{ Goss, Michael R.,	" Oct. 11, 1886		
1851	C	{ Goss, Mrs. Martha E.,			
1877	L	Goss, Mrs. Sarah E.,			
1739		Goodell, Anna,		Died	
1745		Grandee, Elizabeth,		"	
1822		Grant Amos,			
1757		Grant, Eliza,			
1686		Grant, Francis,			
1765		Grant, Lucy,			
1877	L	{ Grant, Deacon Richard T.,			
1877	L	{ Grant, Mrs. Hannah E., (Caswell)			
1744		Grant, Sarah,		Died	
1716		Grant, Susannah,		"	
1843		Graves, Crispus,		"	1863
1843		Graves, Hannah,		"	
1866	C	Graves, Mrs. Lucinda, Died Feb. 20, 1881			
1839		Graves, Mary,		Died	
1843		Graves, Mary A.,		"	
1846		Graves, Ruth E.,			
1877	C	Graves, Susie D.,			
1812		Green, John,		Died	

1737		Green, Mary,	Died
1796		Green, Mary,	"
1828		Green, Rachel,	"
1852		Green, Sarah G.,	Dis.
1881	C	Greene, Mary A.,	
1843		Greene, Jno.,	Died
1825		Greenleaf, Alfred,	"
1767		Greenwood, Mary,	"
1894	C	Gregory, Mrs. Carrie M. (Goldthwait)	
1850		Gregory, Helen M.,	Dis.
1850		⎧ Gregory, James J. H.,	
1877	L	⎨ Gregory, Mrs. Lillie S., (Caswell)	
1887	L	⎩ Gregory, Mrs. Harriet B.,	Died 1894
1876	C	⎰ Gregory, Joseph,	
1871	C	⎱ Gregory, Mrs. Hannah H.,	
1849		Gregory, Mary,	Dis.
1873	L	Gregory, Mrs. Mary,	Dis. Oct. 1877
1832		Gregory, Ruth,	Died
1871	C	Gregory, Mrs. Sarah E.,	
1850		Gregory, Walter R.,	Dis.
1866	C	Griffeth, Mrs. Sarah R.,	
1765		Griffin, Deborah,	Died
1785		Griffin, Martha,	"
1742		Griffin, Mary,	
1770		Griffiths, Sarah,	
1701		Gross, Richard,	"
1871	C	Grove, Mrs. Alice H., (Boardman)	Dis.
1786		Grush, John,	Died
1781		Grush, Sarah,	"

1726		Hadden, Deborah,	Died
1795		Hadley, Martha,	"
1784		Hale, Rebecca,	
1751		Hales, Elizabeth,	
1771		Halfpenny, Margaret,	
1896	L	{ Hall, Herbert J.,	
1894	C	{ Hall, Mrs. Eliza P., (Goldthwait)	
1876	C	Hamelin, Carrie L.,	
1733		Hammilton, Mary,	Died
1810		Hammond, Abagail,	"
1892	L	Hammond, Annie B.,	
1852		Hammond, Caroline B.,	Dis.
1803		Hammond, Deborah,	Died
1742		Hammond, Elenor,	"
1728		Hammond, Elizabeth,	
1752		Hammond, Elizabeth,	
1819		Hammond, Elizabeth,	"
1892	L	Hammond, Mrs. Emma,	Died 1901
1876	C	Hammond, Fred E.,	
1783		Hammond, Hannah,	Died
1789		Hammond, Hannah,	"
1793		Hammond, Jane,	
1818		Hammond, Jane,	
1825		Hammond, Jane,	
1818		Hammond, John,	
1826		Hammond, John,	"
1843		Hammond, John, Jr.,	Ex.
1783		Hammond, Mary,	Died
1800		Hammond, Mary,	"
1825		Hammond, Rebecca E.,	

1877	L	Hammond, Mrs. Sebra,	
1820		Hammond, William D.,	Died
1851	C	Handy, Mrs. Harriet H., (Snow)	Dis. 1886
1684		Hanniford, Miriam,	Died
1710 ·		Hanniford, Miriam,	"
1774		Hanover, Hannah,	
1818		Harding, Mary,	"
1850		Hart, Sarah E.,	Dis.
1815		Harris, Betsy,	Died
1833		Harris, Elizabeth L.,	"
1728		Harris, James,	
1765		Harris, Jean,	
1811		Harris, John,	
1834		Harris, John,	" 1853
1843		Harris, Joseph,	
1847		Harris, Martha,	
1728		Harris, Mary,	
1756		Harris, Mary,	
1834		Harris, Miriam,	
1763		Harris, William,	
1895	C	Hathaway, Mrs. Gertrude M.,	
1871	C	Hathaway, Mrs. Lucretia M., (Clemmons)	
			Died Apr. 20, 1888
1728		Haskal, Susannah,	Died
1866		Haskell, Miriam,	"
1828	C	Hawkes, Ann,	Died July 16, 1878
1832	C	Hawkes, James B.,	" Aug. 21, 1877
1830	C	Hawkes, Mrs. Mary C.,	Died Mar., 1877
1818		Hawkes, Jerusha,	Died
1843		Hawkes, Judith,	"

1875	C	Hawkes, Mrs. Martha A.,	
1885	C	Hawkes, Mary J.,	
1886	C	Hawkes, S. Lizzie,	
1891	C	Hawkes, James W.,	
1685		Hawkins, Agnes,	Died
1728		Hawkins, Mary,	"
1684		Hawley, Johanna,	
1750		Hawley, Margaret,	
1792		Hawley, Martha,	
1727		Hawley, Mary,	
1756		Hawley, Mary,	
1726		Hawley, Richard,	
1783		Hayden, William,	
1718		Hayes, Abagail,	
1718		Hayes, William,	
1702		Haynes, Elizabeth,	
1692		Hayter, Hannah,	
1810		Heath, Annie,	
1810		Heath, Samuel W.,	
1754		Hendley, Abagail,	
1746		Hendley, Deliverance,	
1765		Hendley, Mary,	
1778		Hendley, Mary,	
1739		Hendly, Benjamin,	
1728		Hendly, Elias,	
1728		Hendly, Hannah,	
1720		Hendly, John, Jr.,	
1722		Hendly, Joseph,	
1773		Hendly, Margaret,	
1722		Hendly, Mary,	

1739	Hendly, Mary,	Died
1684	Henly, Sarah,	"
1693	Henly, Sarah, Jr.,	
1701	Henly, Sarah,	
1885 L	Herrick, Mrs. Joanna C.,	
1751	Heyter, Elizabeth,	Died
1717	Hillier, George,	"
1834	Hiller, John C.,	Dis.
1828	Hiller, Mary, .	Died
1738	Hills, Mary,	"
1739	Hind, Alice,	
1718	Hinde, Mary,	
1720	Hindee, Ruth,	
1684	Hinds, Abagail,	
1706	Hinds, Constance,	
1714	Hinds, Elizabeth,	
1803	Hodgkins, Abagail,	"
1850	Holbrook, Mary H.,	Dis.
1888 C	Holden, Mrs. Alice, (Woolston)	
1829	Holden, Martha,	Died
1729	Holman, Elizabeth,	"
1728	Holman, Huldah,	
1761	Holman, Mary,	
1705	Holman, Samuel,	
1713	Homans, Abagail,	
1811	Homan, Abagail,	
1744	Homan, Clattery,	
1811	Homan, Elizabeth,	
1858	{ Homan, Joseph W.,	
1858	{ Homan, Mary W.,	

1702	Homan, Hannah,	Died
1744	Homan, Hannah,	"
1746	Homan, Hannah,	
1819	Homan, Hannah,	
1784	Homan, Joseph,	
1772	Homan, Margaret,	
1705	Homan, Mary,	
1727	Homan, Mary,	
1746	Homan, Mary,	
1882 C	Homan, Mary E.,	
1819	Homan, Nancy,	Died
1795	Homan, Priscilla,	"
1778	Homan, Rebekah,	
1810	Homan, Richard, Jr.,	
1740	Homan, Sarah,	
1785	Homan, Sarah,	
1810	Homan, Sarah,	
1819	Homan, Tabitha,	
1730	Hood, Jennet,	
1820	Hood, Sophia,	
1726	Hooper, Abagail,	
1825	Hooper, Abagail,	
1685	Hooper, Christian,	
1820	Hooper, Deliverance,	
1821	Hooper, Deliverance,	
1761	Hooper, Dorcas,	
1831	Hooper, Eliza,	
1818	Hooper, Elizabeth,	
1849	Hooper, Elizabeth G.,	
1825	Hooper, Eunice,	

1843	Hooper, George,	Died
1738	Hooper, Hannah,	"
1825	Hooper, Hannah,	
1826	Hooper, Hannah,	
1830	Hooper, Hannah,	
1831	Hooper, Hannah,	
1826	Hooper, Hannah G.,	
1857	Hooper, Harriet,	"
1877 L	Hooper, Mrs. Harriet, Died July 10, 1881	
1818	Hooper, Jacob,	Died
1736	Hooper, John, Jr.,	"
1742	Hooper, Joseph,	
1832	Hooper, Louisa,	
1825	Hooper, Lydia,	
1829	Hooper, Martha,	
1738	Hooper, Mary,	
1765	Hooper, Mary,	"
1877 L	Hooper, Mary S.,	Died July 12, 1882
1831	Hooper, Nancy,	Dis.
1825	Hooper, Nathaniel L.,	Died
1821	Hooper, Polly,	"
1763	Hooper, Priscilla,	
1731	Hooper, Rebekah,	
1829	Hooper, Rebecca,	
1729	Hooper, Robert, Jr.,	
1742	Hooper, Ruth,	
1826	Hooper, Sarah,	
1809	Hooper, Sarah Abbot,	
1754	Hooper, Susannah,	
1787	Hooper, Susannah,	

1830		Horton, Emma,	Dis.	
1728		Howard, Nehemiah,	Died	
1685		Hoyle, Anna,	"	
1706		Hoyle, Dorcas,		
1784		Hubbard, Abagail,		
1783		Hubbard, Ebenezer,		
1806		Hubbard, Ebenezer,		
1754		Hudson, Sarah,		
1828		Hulen, Mary,		
1810		Hulen, Sarah,		
1881	C	Humphrey, Caroline E.,		
1832	C	Humphrey, Mrs. Hannah D.,	Died	1881
1874	C	Humphrey, Mrs. Hannah H.,		
1866	C	Humphrey, Mrs. Margaret,	Died	1882
1829	C	Humphrey, Mrs. Mary,	"	1890
1876	C	Humphrey, Mrs. Mary E.,		
1886	C	Humphrey, Mrs. Mary Elizabeth,		
1857	C	Humphrey, Mrs. Rachel F.,	Died	1897
1694		Humphreys, Elizabeth,	"	
1885	L	Humphreys, Mrs. Emily O.,	Dis.	1890
1723		Humphries, Edward,	Died	
1843		Humphries, Edward,	"	
1827		Humphries, John,		
1819		Humphries, Martha,		
1829		Humphries, Sally,		
1803		Humphries, Sarah,		
1885	C	Hunt, Mrs. Hattie,		
1701		Hutchins, Sarah,	Died	
1884	C	Hyam, Mary,		
1843		Hyam, Richard,	Died	1857

1843		Hyam, Richard, Jr.,	Died	1850
1832	C	Hyam, Mrs. Mary,	Died Sept. 5,	1889
1832		Hyde, Margaret,	Died	

1826		Ingalls, Hannah,	Died	
1826		Ingalls, Hannah L.,	"	
1834		Ingalls, John,	"	1860
1685		Ingalls, Mary,	Dis.	
1871	C	Ingalls, Mary,	"	1886
1876	C	Ingalls, Mrs. Mary H., (Conway)		
1877	C	Ingalls, Thomas,	Died July 8,	1887
1793		Ireson, Elizabeth,	Died	
1825		Ireson, Elizabeth,	"	
1839		Ireson, Margaret,		
1711		Ireson, Rebecca,		
1774		Ireson, Sarah,		
1859	C	Ireson, Susan,		
1742		Ivyruy, Anna,	Died	

1744		Jackson, Sarah,	Died	
1725		Jacobs, Abagail,	"	
1728		James, Benjamin,		
1727		James, Hannah,		
1787		James, Mary,		
1740		Jeames, Sarah,		
1829		Johnson, Eleazar,		
1809		Johnson, John,		
1866		Johnson, Mahitable,		
1778		Johnson, Mary,		
1850		Jones, Dorothy,		
1728		Jones, William,		

1866	C	Keating, Mrs. Mary,	Died Nov., 1888
1819		Kelley, Hepsibah,	Died
1858		Kimball, Emeline,	"
1825		Kimball, Mary,	
1739		King, Elizabeth,	
1821		King, Elizabeth,	
1876	C	King, Giles,	
1738		King, Samuel,	Died
1896		King, Mrs. Sarah W.,	
1772		King, Thomas,	Died
1747		Kitchens, Hannah,	"
1830		Kitchens, Hannah,	
1829		Kitchens, Samuel,	"
1878	C	⎰ Knight, Deacon Benj. F.,	Died 1886
1878	C	⎱ Knight, Mrs. Caroline,	
1876	C	Knight, Mrs. Carrie C.,	Died 1897
1730		Knight, Deliverance,	"
1728		Knight, Ebenezer,	
1725		Knight, Elizabeth,	
1806		Knight, Elizabeth,	
1818		Knight, Elizabeth,	
1825		Knight, Elizabeth,	
1843		Knight, Elizabeth,	"
1868	C	Knight, Mrs. Eliza M.,	Died Nov. 3, 1881
1830		Knight, Emma,	Died
1843	C	Knight. Mrs. Hannah G.,	" 1898
1726		Knight, Jean,	"
1843		Knight, John,	Dis.
1871	C	Knight, Lizzie M.,	
1752		Knight, Mary,	Died

1788	Knight, Ruth,	Died	
1832	Knight, Samuel,	"	
1871 C	Knight, Sarah,		
1844	Knight, Susan G.,	Dis.	
1788	Knight, William,	Died	
1687	Knott, Hannah,	"	
1847 L	Knowland, Richardson,	"	1895
1822	Lackey, Andrew,	Died	
1818	Lackey, Mary,	"	
1820	{ Lambord, Rev. Benj. F.,		
1820	{ Lambord, Polly,		
1830	Lamprell, Hannah,		
1882 C	Lancey, Lizzie H.,		
1828	Langley, Elizabeth,	Died	
1843	Lane, Sarah W.,	"	
1729	Laskey, Elizabeth,		
1788	Laskey, Elizabeth,		
1742	Laskey, Jonas,		
1729	Laskey, Mary,		
1692	Laskey, Robert,		
1826	Laskey, Sarah,		
1788	Laskey, Thomas,		
1742	Laskey, William,		
1760	Lathrope, Judith,		
1877 L	{ LAWRENCE, REV. EDWARD A.,	"	1883
1845	{ Lawrence, Mrs. Margaret W.	Dis.	
1838	Lawrence, Mary,	Died	
1850	Leavitt, Hannah,	"	
1843	{ Lecraw, David R.,	"	1873
1830	{ Lecraw, Mrs. Hannah R.,	"	1899

70

1819		Lecraw, John,	Died	
1818		Lecraw, Rebecca,	"	
1825		Lecraw, Rebecca,		
1763		⎰ Lee, Jeremiah, Esquire,		
1747		⎱ Lee, Martha,		
1751		Lee, Sarah,		
1770		Leech, Deborah,		
1856		Lefavour, Lucy J. M.,	"	
1684		Legg, Elizabeth,	Dis.	
1766		Legrow, Anna,	Died	
1772		LeMastin, Thomas,	"	
1884	C	Lemaster, Mrs. Mary E.,		
1743		Lemmon, Joseph,	Died	
1819		Lewis, Charlotte,	"	
1865	C	Lewis, Mrs. Deborah,	"	1889
1800		Lewis, Lydia,		
1716		Ley, John,		
1716		Ley, Mary,		
1717		Le'Vallie, Sarah,		
1886	C	Lindsey, Amy B.,		
1897	C	Lindsey, Deliverance B.,		
1850	C	Lindsey, Mrs. Emily S., (Blaney)		
1884	C	Lindsey, Mrs. Georgie A., (Martin)		
1843		Lindsey, Lois,	Died	1860
1811		Lindsey, Mary,	"	
1811		Lindsey, Sarah,		
1816		Lindsey, Sarah,		
1876		Lindsey, Mrs. Sarah L.,		
1871	C	⎰ Litchman, William T.,	Died	1895
1871		⎱ Litchman, Mrs. Sarah,		

71

1829	Longley, Nancy,	Died	
1819	Lovett, Hannah,	"	
1740	Lovis, Mary,		
1773	Lovis, Susanna,		
1772	Lowell, John,		
1760	Lowell, Sarah,		
1690	Luckers, Jemina,		
1737	Lyndsey, Joseph,		
1818	Lyon, Rebecca,		
1829	Lyon, Rebecca,		
1830	Lyon, Sarah,		
1829	Lyons, Hannah,		
1803	Mann, Ruth,	Died	
1834	Manning, Eleanor N.,	"	
1827	Manning, Elizabeth,		
1850 C	Manning, Mrs. Elizabeth W.,	"	
1843	Manning, Mary A., ·		
1827	Manning, Samuel,		
1843	Manning, William S.,		
1741	Marshall, Eliza.,		
1878 L	Martin, Abbie B.,	"	1899
1698	Martin, Elizabeth,	Dis.	
1783	Martin, Elizabeth,	Died	
1831	Martin, Hannah,	"	
1874 C	Martin, Mrs. Hannah B.,		
1832	Martin, Jane,	Died	
1843 C	Martin, Mrs. Jane,	"	1887
1787	Martin, Knott, Jr.,		
1885 C	Martin, Mrs. Mary Ann,	"	1890

1850	C Martin, Mrs. Mary B.,		
1786	Martin, Mercy,	Died	
1832	Martin, Samuel,	"	
1756	Martin, Sarah,		
1786	Martin, Sarah,		
1876	C Martin, Mrs. Sarah J.,		
1752	Martyn, Eleanor,	Died	
1737	Masury, Eliza,	"	
1706	Matthews, Elizabeth,		
1684	Maverick, Eunice,		
1684	Maverick, Moses,		
1719	Mayfield, Samuel,		
1849	McCauley, Jane.	"	
1872	McCullough, Mary,	Dis.	
1850	⎧ McEachran, Collin,	Died	1895
1850	⎨ McEachran, Mrs. Eliza,	"	1879
1882	L ⎩ McEachran, Mrs. Euphemia,	Dis.	
1830	McIntire, Elizabeth,	Died	
1770	McIntire, Lydia.	"	
1830	McIntire, Samuel T.,		
1877	L McPhale, Mrs. Agnes,	"	1890
1715	Meek, Elizabeth,		
1835	Meek, Hannah,		
1825	Meek, Mary,		
1747	Mecholly, Mary,		
1700	Meirs, Abagail,		
1819	Merrill, Eleanor,		
1819	Merrill, Joseph,		
1684	Merritt, Abagail,		
1731	Merritt, Anna,		

1728		Merritt, Charity,	Died
1697		Merritt, Elizabeth,	"
1729		Merritt, Elizabeth,	"
1876	C	Merritt, Carrie E.,	Dis.
1728		Merritt, Jean,	Died
1729		Merritt, Jean,	"
1684		Merritt, John,	
1706		Merritt, John,	
1684		Merritt, Mary,	
1684		Merritt, Mary,	
1736		Merritt, Mary,	
1825		Merritt, Mary,	"
1830		Merritt, Mary W.,	Dis.
1728		Merritt, Nicholas, Sen.,	Died
1729		Merritt, Nicholas, 3d,	"
1684		Merritt, Sarah,	
1706		Merritt, Sarah,	
1742		Merritt, Sarah,	
1830		Merritt, Sarah,	
1786		Melzard, Mary,	
1803		Melzard, Mary,	
1886	C	Melzard, Mrs. Mary B.,	
1825		Melzard, Sally,	Died
1723		Merry, Judith,	"
1787		Miles, Susannah,	
1818		Miller, Jona. P.,	
1891	C	Mitchell, Cora L.,	
1877	L	Mitchell, Mrs. Elizabeth C.,	
1756		Mooney, Susannah,	Died
1838		Moore, Elizabeth C.,	"

1728		Morris, Mary,	Died
1704		Moss, Christian,	"
1765		Mugford, Lydia,	
1737		Mullett, Thomas,	"
1880	L	Munroe, Rev. Egbert N.,	Dis.
1877	L	Munroe, Mrs. Marianna.,	
1885	L	Munroe, Michael B.,	Died 1892
1727		Murray, Daniel,	"
1882	C	Murray, Mrs. Lizzie A., (Jepson) Dis.	

1871	C	Neilson, Mrs. Mary A. B., (Harris)	
1698		Nerdan, Nathanal,	Died
1689		Newberry, Martha,	"
1832		Newhall, Joel,	
1819		Newhall, Mary,	
1820		Newhall, Sally,	
1832		Newhall, Sarah,	"
1855		Nichols, Mary,	Dis.
1692		Nicholson, Elizabeth,	Died
1716		Nicholson, Eliza.,	"
1741		Nicholson, Emma,	
1776		Nicholson, Emma,	
1734		Nicholson, Lydia,	
1720		Nicholson, Martha,	
1728		Nicholson, Martha,	
1735		Nicholson, Mary,	
1701		Nicholson, Robeit,	
1720		Nicholson, Robert,	"
1835		{ NILES, REV. M. A. H.,	Ex.
1839		{ Niles, Stella S.,	"

1877	L	Nims, Mrs. Anna D.,	Dis.
1706		Norden, Mrs. Jane,	Died
1685		Norman, Margaret,	"
1871	C	North, Mary E.,	Dis.
1875	C	North, Mrs. Mary S.,	
1866		{ Noyes, Abbie M.,	Dis.
1866		{ Noyes, J. H.,	"
1850		Nutting, Eliza S.,	"
1745		Nutting, Mary,	Died
1838	C	Nutting, Mrs. Mary,	" 1889
1747		Oaks, Abagail,	Died
1876	C	Oliver, Mrs. Mary E.,	
1733		Oliver, Thomas,	Died
1712		Olton, Deborah,	"
1739		Orn, Joshua, Jr.,	
1739		Orn, Sarah,	
1786		Orne, Hon. Azor, Esq.,	" 1799
1714		Orne, Elizabeth,	
1714		Orne, Joshua,	
1820	C	Orne, Mrs. Margaret,	" 1879
1751		Orne, Mary,	
1751		Orne, Simon,	
1820		Osborn, Elizabeth,	
1716		Owen, Grace,	
1703		Owens, Martha,	
1776		Page, Abagail,	Died
1739		Page, Hannah,	"
1715		Palmer, Mary,	

1883	L	Parker, Mrs. Annie W.,		
1712		Parker, David,	Died	
1716		Parker, Hepsibah,	"	
1716		Parker, Judith,		
1716		Parker, Thomas,		
1684		Parmiter, Benjamin,		
1751		Patten, John,		
1805		Patten, Elizabeth,		
1843		Patten, Mary B.,		
1838		Patten, Mary,		
1728		Patten, Sarah,		
1789		Peach, Elizabeth,	"	
1851	C	Peach, Mrs. Elizabeth S.,	Dis.	
1687		Peach, Emma,	Died	
1740		Peach, Emma,	"	
1789		Peach, John,		
1741		Peach, Mary,		
1785		Peach, Mary,		
1714		Peach, Sarah,		
1763		Peach, Sarah,		
1762		Peach, William,		
1719		Peak, Esther,		
1684		Pederick, Dorcas,		
1729		Pederick, Jean,		
1699		Pederick, Mary,		
1684		Pederick, Miriam,		
1728		Pederick, Richard,		
1819		Pedrick, Abagail,		
1877	L	Pedrick, Mrs. Abigail B.,	"	1885
1824		Pedrick, Ann,		

1843	Pedrick, Eliza.,	Died	
1817	Pedrick, Elizabeth,	"	
1850 C	Pedrick, Mrs. Elizabeth H.,		
1850 C	Pedrick, Elizabeth S.,	Died	1881
1877 L	Pedrick, Mrs. Carrie E.,		
1819	Pedrick, Hannah,	Died	
1700	Pedrick, John,	"	
1848	Pedrick, John,		
1843	Pedrick, Knott,	"	1880
1771	Pedrick, Mary,		
1827	Pedrick, Mary,		
1849	Pedrick, Mary Rebecca,		
1832	Pedrick, Mrs. Sarah H.,	"	1892
1843	Pedrick, Thomas,		
1843	Pedrick, Thomas B.,	"	1854
1766	Pepper, Lydia,		
1874 C	Perkins, Mrs. Hannah,		
1818	Perry, Susanna,	Died	
1843	Pettingell, Ephraim,	"	
1730	Pew, Phillis,		
1811	Phelps, John,		
1746	Phillips, Eliza.,		
1762	Phillips, Eliza.,	"	
1843	Phillips, Eliza L,	Dis.	
1827	Phillips, Deliverance,	"	
1718	Phillips, Hipsibah,	Died	
1843	Phillips, Ichabod,	"	
1819	Phillips, Ichabod S.,	Dis.	
1718	Phillips, Jona.,	Died	
1825	Phillips, Nancy,	Dis.	

1877	L	Phillips, Mrs. Nancy,	Died	1878
1832		Phillips, Robert,	Dis.	
1739		Phillips, Sarah,	Died	
1736		Phillips, Steven,	"	
1697		Pickett, Mary,		
1684		Pickworth, Abagail,		
1743		Pickworth, Mary,	"	
1884	C	Pierce, Alice C.,	Dis.	
1858	C	⎰ Pierce, Deacon Benj. F.,	"	
	C	⎱ Pierce, Mrs. Mary R.,		
1866		Pierce, Deborah,	"	
1830	C	Pierce, Mrs. Emma,	Died	1885
1843	C	⎰ Pierce, George,	"	1884
1825	C	⎱ Pierce, Mrs. Deborah,	"	1878
1853		Pierce, George, Jr.,	Dis.	
1698		Pierce, Mary,	Died	
1724		Pierce, Mary,	"	
1877	C	Pierce, Mrs. Sarah E.,		
1850	C	Pierce, Sarah H.,	Died	1891
1802		Pierce, Tabitha,	"	
1727		Pierson, James,		
1719		Pierson, Mary,		
1696		Piper, Grace,		
1866		Pitman, Abby,		
1684		Pitman, Charity,		
1702		Pitman, Elizabeth,		
1741		Pitman, Hannah,		
1684		Pitman, Jane,		
1684		Pitman, John,		
1731		Pitman, Margaret,		

1728		Pitman, Martha,	Died
1713		Pitman, Mary,	"
1787		Pitman, Mary,	
1871	C	Pitman, Mrs. Mary E.,	
1743		Pitman, Rachael,	Died
1684		Pitman, Thomas, Sen.,	"
1687		Pitman, Thomas, Jun.,	
1719		Pittman, John,	
1728		Pittman, Mary,	
1729		Pittman, Sarah,	
1875	C	Pope, Mrs. Emeline R.,	
1877	C	{ Pope, George G.,	
1876	C	{ Pope, Mrs. Carrie A.,	
1803		Porter, Deliverance,	Died
1834		Porter, Samuel A.,	Ex.
1843		Porter, Sophronia,	"
1783		Pote, Capt. Samuel,	Died
1900	C	Potter, Alice Jeannette,	
1898	C	Potter, Mrs. Lillie, (Foss)	
1788		Pousland, Abagail,	Died
1770		Pousland, Elizabeth,	"
1728		Pousland, Tabitha,	
1736		Pousland, Thomas,	"
1874		Powell, Annie E.,	Dis.
1888	C	Power, Mrs. A. Maria,	
1710		Powsland, Grace,	Died
1810		Pratt, Jonathan,	"
1886	C	Pratt, Lucina H.,	
1882	L	Pray, Mrs. Cora E.,	Dis.
1834		Preble, John B.,	Died

1742	Preble, Sarah,	Died	
1838	Prentiss, Eleanor H.,	"	
1818	Prentiss, Elizabeth,		
1830	Prentiss, Ellen H.,	"	
1850	Prentiss, Mary E.,	Dis.	
1804	Prentiss, Sarah,	Died	
1850 C	Prentiss, Mrs. Sarah A.,	"	1894
1880 C	Priest, Eugenia R.,	Dis.	
1762	Prince, Anna,	Died	
1807	Prince, Hannah,	"	
1795	Prince, Joseph,		
1822	Prince, Sarah,		
1756	Pritchard, Charity,	"	
1850	Pritchard, Harriet A.,	Dis.	
1832	Procter, Eliza,	"	
1832	Procter, John,	Died	
1726	Procter, Kesiah,	"	
1783	Procter, Nancy,		
1721	Procter, Sarah,		
1738	Procter, Tabitha,		
1874 C	Proctor, Hattie R.,	"	1892
1823	Proctor, Mary I.,		
1825	Putnam, Ann,		
1839	{ Quill, David,	Died	
1843 C	{ Quill, Mrs. Hannah B.,	"	1893
1820	Quill, Sally,	"	
1850	Quiner, Deborah H.,	Dis.	
1791	Quiner, Elizabeth,	Died	
1843	Quiner, Jane,	"	

81

1877	L	Rand, Mrs. Carrie T.,	Dis.	
1877	L	Ramsdell, Mrs. Carrie C., (Tindley)		
1844		Ramsdell, George,	Died	1855
1884	C	Ramsdell, Mrs. Mary A., .		
1832		Ramsdell, Sarah,	Died	
1834		Ramsdell, Susannah,	"	
1843		Ramsdell, Sarah,	Ex.	
1716		Raymond, Eunice,	Died	
1829		. Reed, Lucy Ann,	"	
1700		Reed, Mary.		
1825		Reed, Mary,	"	
1832		Reed, Mary, .	Dis.	
1820		Reed, Rebecca,	Died	
1830		Reed, Rebecca,	Dis.	
1823		{ Reed, William,	Died	1837
1831		{ Reed, Hannah,	"	1855
1727		Reith, Abagail,		
1692		Reith, Ann,		
1713		Reith, Anna,		
1719		Reith, Isabella,		
1742		Reith, Lydia,		
1684		Reith, Richard,		
1713		Reith, Richard,		
1714		Reith, William,		
1851		Reynolds, Eliza,		
1725		Rhodes, Eleanor,		
1717		Rhodes, Margaret,		
1723		Rhodes, Miriam,		
1695		Rhodes, Samuel,		
1728		Rhodes, Sarah,		

1764	Richardson, Eliza,	Died	
1839	Richardson, John,	Dis.	
1727	Richardson, Margaret,	Died	
1742	Richardson, Mary,	"	
1829	Rideout, Sumner,	Dis.	
1727	Riddan, Jerusha,	Died	
1719	Riddan, Sarah,	"	
1875 C	Rix, Mrs. Mary A.,	"	1889
1684	Road, Edward,	"	
1884 C	Roads, Mrs. Martha D., (Ramsdell)		
1703	Roads, Elizabeth, ₄	Died	
1706	Roads, Tabitha,	"	
1804	Robinson, Anna,		
1804	Robinson, Benjamin,		
1810	Robinson, Bezer,		
1742	Robinson, Eliza.,		
1837 C	Robinson, Sally,	"	1882
1713	Rockwood, John,		
1685	Rogers, Abraham,		
1819	Rogers, Caroline, .		
1884 C	Rogers, M. Lizzie,		
1843 C	Rogers, Deacon Peter J.,	Died	1880
1684	Rolls, Mary,	"	
1716	Rolls, Mary,		
1804	Ropes, Mary,		
1793	Ross, Alexander,		
1785	Ross, Rebecca,		
1784	Ross, Sarah,		
1821	Ross, Sarah,		
1741	Roundy, Desire,		

1819	Roundy, Desire,	Died
1810	Roundy, Elizabeth,	"
1784	Roundy, Eunice,	
1742	Roundy, John,	
1790	Roundy, Jonathan,	
1897 C	Roundy, Mrs. Lizzie Maria,	
1832	Roundy, Sally,	Dis.
1834	Roundy, Sarah,	"
1810	Roundey, Elijah,	Died
1828	Roundey, Ruth,	Dis.
1741	Roundey,·Thomas,	Died
1812	Roundey, Thomas,	"
1894 C	Rouse, Thomas A.,	
1743	Row, Sussannah,	Died
1889 C	Rowe, Sarah S., (Hammond)	Dis.
1708	Rowles, Elizabeth,	Died
1834	Rundlett, Sarah,	"
1829 C	Russell, Mrs. Abigail,	" 1890
1850	Russell, Caroline W.,	Dis.
1742	Russell, Dorcas,	Died
1684	Russell, Elizabeth,	"
1684	Russell, Elizabeth,	
1705	Russell, Elizabeth,	
1734	Russell, Giles,	
1819	Russell, Hannah,	
1888 C	Russell, Hattie,	
1714	Russell, Henry,	· Died
1819	Russell, John,	"
1771	Russell, Martha,	
1684	Russell, Mary,	

1687	Russell, Mary,	Died
1811	Russell, Mary,	"
1825	Russell, Mary,	
1832	Russell, Mary Ann H.,	
1825	Russell, Peter Edmund,	
1819	Russell, Polly,	
1714	Russell, Rebecca,	"
1854	Russell, Ruth,	Dis.
1843	Russell, Sally,	Died
1714	Russell, Sarah,	"
1726	Russell, Sarah,	
1861	Russell, Sarah,	"
1819	Rust, Samuel,	Dis.
1737	Salkeld, Sarah,	Died
1810	Salkins, Martha,	"
1741	Salter, Eliza.,	
1738	Salter, Margaret,	
1732	Salter, Sarah,	"
1871	C Sanborn, Mrs. Lizzie H., (Bateman) Dis.	
1852	L Sanborn, Nathan P.,	
1876	C Sanborn, N. Willard,	Dis.
1701	Sanders, Charity,	Died
1684	Sandin, Charity,	"
1695	Sandin, Ephraim,	
1720	Sandin, Ephraim, Jr.,	
1695	Sandin, Miriam,	
1719	Sandin, Miriam,	
1684	Sandin, Sumuel,	
1763	Sanson, Susannah,	

1735	Saunders, Jean,	Died	
1718	Saunders, Sarah,	"	
1810	Savage, Sarah,		
1876 C	Savory, Abbie B.,		
1900 C	Savory, Arthur F.,		
1877 L	⎰ Savory, Deacon Benjamin,		
1874 C	⎱ Savory, Mrs. Sarah E.,		
1858	Savory, Elizabeth D.,	Died	
1855 C	Savory, Mrs. Hannah,		
1858	Savory, John H.,	Died	1862
1858 C	Savory, Mrs. Mary W.,	"	1882
1731	Scammon, Sarah,		
1731	Scammon, Thomas,		
1765	Sciverey, Mary,		
1835	Scivery, Benjamin,		
1810	Scivery, Sarah,		
1810	Scivery, Sarah,		
1818	Scivery, Sarah,		
1723	Scolly, Elizabeth,		
1717	Scolly, John, Jr.,		
1834	Scores, Abagail V.,		
1756	Searl, Deliverance,		
1706	Searle, Lydia,		
1889 C	Seavey, Walter M.,	"	1893
1695	Seaward, Johana,		
1692	Seaward, Susanna,		
1792	Seawood, Mary,		
1802	Selman, Abagail,		
1832	Selman, Abagail,		
1744	Selman, Archebald,		

1743	Selman, Eliza.,	Died	
1830	Selman, Eliza,	"	1897
1818	Selman, Elizabeth,		
1825	Selman, Esther,		
1820	Selman, Francis G.,		
1805	Selman, Hannah,		
1747	Selman, Joseph, Jr.,		
1830	Selman, Mary Jane,		
1784	Selman, Patience,		
1746	Selman, Sarah,		
1829	Selman, Sarah,		
1684	Seyward, John,		
1724	Shapley, Mary,		
1885 C	Shattuck, Charles H.,		
1885 L	Shattuck, Mrs. Ellen,		
1838	Shaw, Sarah,	Died	
1726	Shelden, Isabella,	"	
1885 C	Shepard, Annie,		
1838	Shepard, Augusta,	Ex.	
1866 C	Silver, Mrs. Martha,	Died	1889
1834	Simpson, David S.,	"	1856
1849	Simpson, Margaret,		
1833 C	Simpson, Mrs. Sally K.,	"	1884
1832	Sivery, Mary,		
1719	Skillen, Mary,		
1728	Skilling, Nehemiah,	"	
1692	Skinner, Alice,	Dis.	
1705	Skinner, Richard,	"	
1830	Smetherst, Hannah,	Died	
1897 C	Smethurst, Jennie B.,		

1871	C Smethurst, Lizzie T.,		
1863	L Smethurst, Mrs. Mary J.,		
1819	Smith, Clarrissa,	Died	
1743	Smith, Deliverance,	"	
1773	Smith, Elizabeth,		
1684	Smith, Hannah,	"	
1855	Smith, J. F.,	Dis.	
1810	Smith, Mary,	Died	
1874	C Smith, Mrs. Mary E.,		
1832	C Smith, Mary B.,	Died 1890	
1832	Smith, Mercy A. K.,	"	
1788	Smith, Rebecca,	"	
1866	Snelling, John,	Dis.	
1829	Snow, James,	Died	
1829	C Snow, Mrs. Susan,	"	1879
1850	Snow, Susan,		
1685	Sowdine, Elenor,		
1840	Sparhawk, Louisa,		
1832	Sparhawk, Sarah,		
1754	Stacey, Benjamin,		
1843	Stacey, Eliza,	"	1857
1863	C Stacey, Mrs. Eliza,	"	1871
1825	C Stacey, Mrs. Elizabeth W.,	"	1882
1877	L { Stacey, Girdler,		
1877	L { Stacey, Mrs. Annie B.,		
1843	Stacey, Jno. G.,	Died	
1754	Stacey, Mary,	"	
1802	Stacey, Mary,		
1843	Stacey, Rebecca,	"	1854
1843	Stacey, Rebecca L.,		

1843		Stacey, Sally P.,	Died	
1715		Stacey, Samuel,	Dis.	
1743		Stacey, Samuel,	Died	
1858	C	{ Stacey, William,		
1876	C	{ Stacey, Mrs. Jane,	Died	1889
1685		Stadden, Hannah,	Dis.	
1858	C	Standley, Mrs. Eliza,		
1884	C	Standley, Mrs. Jane B.,	Died	1892
1797		Standley, Margaret,	"	
1733		Standley, Mary,		
1684		Stasey, Agnes,		
1684		Stasey, John,	"	
1701		Stasey, Mary,	Dis.	
1819		Stevens, Betsey,	Died	
1751		Stevens, Eliza,	"	
1850		Stevens, Lucy A. C.,		
1859	C	Stevens, Mrs. Margaret,	"	1894
1810		Stevens, Mary,		
1834		Stevens, Mary Ann,		
1832		Stevens, Rebecca,		
1810		Stevens, Sarah,		
1850		Stevens, S. G.,		
1834		Stevens, Tabitha,		
1731		Stevens, Thomas,		
1858		{ Stevens, Thomas,		
1858	C	{ Stevens, Mrs. Harriet H.,		
1896	L	Stewart, Mrs. Pansy,		
1686		Stilson, Margaret,	Died	
1692		Stilson, Sarah,	"	
1861		Stocks, Elizabeth,	Dis.	

1886 L Stoddard, Carrie E.,
1886 L Stoddard, Mary R.,
1886 L Stoddard, Samuel P.,
1898 C (Stone, Andrew M.,
1898 C (Stone, Mrs. Eleanor P., (Chamberlin)
1865   (Stone, Henry,   Dis.
1865   (Stone, Mrs. Lois H.,   "
1858 C (Stone, Joseph W., ·   Died 1897
1861 L (Stone, Mrs. Ruth A.,
1876 C Stone, Mrs. Mary E.,   Died 1884
1842 C Stone, Mrs. Priscilla W.,
1858   Stone, Mrs. Sarah,   Died 1859
1816   Story, Elizabeth,   "
1719   Striker, Abagail,
1756   Striker, Margaret,
1736   Striker, Miriam,
1756   Striker, Samuel,
1719   Striker, Zachariah,   "
1784   Sturgeon, Miriam,   Died
1843   Sullivan, Margaret,   "
1888 L (Sumner, J. F.,
1888 L (Sumner, Mrs. Mary L.,
1888 L Sumner, Lottie M.,
1888 L Sumner, Maggie L.,
1720   Swan, Rachael,   Died
1737   Swan, Sarah,   "
1738   Swann, Thomas,
1726   Sweat, Martha,
1716   Sweat, Ruth,
1876 C Sweet, Mrs. Elizabeth E.,

1725		Sweet, Joseph	Died	
1690		Swetland, Rebecca	"	
1751		Swett, Anna		
1820		Swett, Ann W.,		
1874	C	Swett, Carrie A.,	"	1891
1828		Swett, Mary B.,		
1811		Swett, Nancy,	"	
1876	C	Swett, Nellie I..,	Dis.	1880
1872	L	Swett, William B.,	Died	1884
1684		Symonds, Anna,	"	
1884	C	Symonds, Annie B.,		

1725		Tawley, John,	Died	
1743		Tawley, Mary,	"	
1704		Taynour, Mary,		
1721		Tewksbury, Henry,		
1795		Tewksbury, Sarah,		
1802		Thompson, Anna,		
1834		Thompson, Elizabeth,		
1807		Thompson, Gabriel,		
1770		Thompson, James,		
1703		Thompson, Jonathan,		
1834		Thompson, Jonathan,	"	1855
1876	C	Thompson, Lizzie,		
1764		Thompson, Margaret,	Died	
1795		Thompson, Margaret,	"	
1796		Thompson, Margaret,		
1703		Thompson, Mary,		
1738		Thompson, Rebekah,		
1877	L	Thompson, Susan,	"	1893

1832		Thompson, Susan,	Dis.	
1825		Thompson, William,	Died	
1891	L	⎧ Tinker, B. W.,	Dis.	
1891	L	⎩ Tinker, Mrs. Lizzie W.,	"	
1877	L	Tindley, Mrs. Margaret,		
1815		Tinley, Anna,	Died	
1851	C	Tishew, Elizabeth,	"	1882
1825	C	Tishew, Mrs. Sally,	"	1881
1818		Topham, Annis,		
1851		Tracy, Mary Ann,	"	
1819		Trask, George,	Dis.	
1892	C	Treen, Mary E.,	"	
1706		Trefry, Annis,	Died	
1764		Trefry, Eliza.,	"	
1783		Trefry, Elizabeth,		
1827		Trefry, Lydia,		
1727		Trefry, Mary,		
1728		Trefry, Rebekah,		
1695		Trefry, Sarah,		
1727		Trefry, Sarah,		
1784		Trefry, Sarah,		
1812		Trefry, Tameson,		
1790		Trefry, Thomas,		
1713		Trevett, Anne,		
1714		Trevett, Elizabeth,		
1714		Trevett, Henry,		
1714		Trevett, John,	"	
1693		Trevett, Martha,	Dis.	
1714		Trevett, Richard,	"	
1714		Trevett, Sarah,		

1730		Trow, Sarah,	Died	
1898	L	True, Charlotte L.,		
1898	L	True, Harry E.,		
1898	L	True, J. Webster,		
1898	L	True, Margaret P.,		
1898	L	{ True, Dr. Richard S.,		
1898	L	{ True, Mrs. Thankful E.,		
1898	L	True, Richard S., Jr.,		
1825		Tucker, Eleanor,	Died	
1858	C	Tucker, Mrs. Ellen M.,	Dis.	
1791		Tucker, Hannah,	Died	
1727		Tucker, Miriam,	"	
1879	C	Tucker, Richard,	"	1884
1858		Tucker, Susan G.,		
1767		Tuexbury, Hannah, Senior,		
1767		Tuexbury, Hannah,	"	
1830		Turell, Jane,	Dis.	
1832		Turell, Martha Ann,	Died	
1728		Turner, Isaac,	"	
1728		Turner, Mary,		
1772		Turner, Samuel,		
1842		{ Turner, William O.,	"	1863
1842		{ Turner, Mrs. Bethiah,	"	1865
1885	C	{ Tutt, Deacon Edward D.,		
1884	C	{ Tutt, Mrs. Sarah W., (Main)		
1850	C	Tutt, Mrs. Hannah,	Died	1893
1874	C	Tutt, Mrs. Hannah A.,		
1884	C	Tutt, Hannah,		
1879	C	Tutt, Mrs. Mary A.,		
1877	C	Tutt, Richard,	Died	1879

1889	C	{ Tutt, Deacon Richard,		
1883	C	{ Tutt, Mrs. Annie C., (Woolston)		
1843		Tutt, William R.,	Died	1869
1823		Twisden, Catherine,	"	
1834		Twisden, Eben S, .		
1827		Twisden, Elizabeth,		
1701		Twisden, Sarah,		

1762	Union, Eliza,	Died	
1812	Union, Elizabeth,	"	
1832	Union, Lydia,	Dis.	
1850	{ Usher, Edward M.,	"	
1850	{ Usher, Rebecca D.,	Died	1888
1877 L	Usher, Mrs. Hattie,		
1886 C	Usher, Mrs. Mattie, (Broughton)		

1876 C	Valentine, Elizabeth,	Died	1897
1850	Valentine, Hannah C.,	"	
1829	Valentine, Mary,		
1838	Valentine, Mary,		
1771	Vickery, Sarah,		

1819	Wadden, Benjamin, Jr.,	Died	
1829	Wadden, Sarah,	"	
1834	Wadden, William,	"	1861
1820	Wait, Charlotte,		
1695	Walbord, Nathaniel,		
1713	Waldron, Deliverance,		
1750	Waldron, Eunice,		
1727	Waldron, Hannah,		

1728	Waldron, John,	Died	
1727	Waldron, Joseph,	"	
1692	Waldron, Miriam,		
1811	Walpee, Mary,		
1684	Ward, Sarah,		
1852	Washburn, Mrs. Sarah G.,		
1684	Watts, Elizabeth,	Died	
1741	Watts, Rachael,	"	
1900 C	Wayland, Frederick,		
1900 C	{ Wayland, Valentine,		
1900 C	{ Wayland, Mrs. Alice,		
1842	Weed, Celestia,	Died	
1825	Weed, Dan,	"	
1834	Weed, Dan, Jr.,		
1825	Weed, Lucy,		
1831	Weed, Lucy,		
1771	Weld, Edward,		
1735	Webber, Hannah,	'	
1877 L	West, Mrs. Lizzie E., (Savory)		
1861 C	West, Mary E.,	Died	1894
1850	Whidden, Catherine T.,	Dis.	
1720	White, Arabella,	Died	
1832	White, Elias,	"	
1832	White, Eliza,		
1707	White, Elizabeth,		
1703	White, John,		
1727	White, Martha,		
1741	White, Mary,		
1810	White, Mary,		
1834	White, Philip H.,	"	1874

1716		White, Remember,	Died	
1819		White, Sarah,	"	
1836	C	White, Susan H.,		
1877	L	Whitmore, Mrs. M. Lizzie,	Dis.	
1763		Whitwell, Prudence,	Died	
1762		WHITWELL, MR. WILLIAM,	"	1781
1834		Williams, Anna,		
1783		Williams, Eleanor,	"	
1873	L	{ WILLIAMS, REV. JOHN H.,	Dis.	
1873	L	{ Williams, Mrs. Annie F.,	"	
1819		Williams, Margaret S.,	Died	
1755		Williams, Mary,	"	
1834		Williams, Mary,		
1853		Williams, Martha C.,		
1754		Williams, William,	"	
1890	C	{ Winslow, Albert H.,	Dis.	
1890	L	{ Winslow, Mrs. Winnie,	"	
1816		Wolcott, Sally,	Died	
1721		Wood, Elizabeth,	"	
1727		Wood, Elizabeth,		
1717		Wood, Thomas,		
1686		Woods, Mary,		
1692		Woods, Tabitha,		
1877	L	Woodfin, Mrs. Caroline,	"	1880
1877	L	Woodfin, Mrs. Margaret A.,		
1831		Woodfin, Sarah,	Died	
1687		Woodley, Elizabeth,	"	
1840		Wooldredge, Eliza,		
1776		Wooldredge, Mary,		
1843		Wooldredge, Mary E.,		

1850   Wooldridge, Eliza,   Died

1802   Wooldridge, Mary,   "

1819   Wooldridge, Rebecca,

1806   Wooldridge, Sarah,

1832   Wooldridge, William,

1888 C Woolston, Ellen E.,

1885 C Woolston, William G.,

1874 C ⎰ Wormstead, Dea. Wm. H.,   Dis.

1874 C ⎱ Wormstead, Mrs. Hattie G., "

List of Members,

1881 C Adams, Mrs. Sarah,

1850 C Appleton, Daniel,

1894 C Atkins, Hannah,   (a)

1892 C Atkins, Nathaniel H.,   Dis. 1901

1874 C Atkins, Rebecca P.,   "   1901

1876 C Bailey, Mary B.,

1888 C Bartlett, Mrs. Cora L., (Tucker)

1871 C Bartol, Mrs. Emma, (Clemmons)

1877 L Barry, Mrs. Dora, (Tindley)   (a)

1876 C Bates, Maria L.,

1884 L { BELL, REV. S. LINTON,

1889 C { Bell, Mrs. Leila E.,

1876 C Bessom, Mrs. Ellen,

1858 C Blackler, Mrs. Mary E.,

1871 C Boardman, Mrs. Susan G.,

1898 C Bragdon, Mrs. Mary Eliza,

1888 C Breare, Mrs. Abbie, (Martin)

1892 C { Brewer, John M.,   (a)

1871 C { Brewer, Mrs. Sarah L., (Doliber) "

1877 C Broughton, Deacon Frank,

1877 C { Broughton, Deacon John G.,

1868 C { Broughton, Mrs. Mary L., (Chamberlin)

1884 C Broughton, Mary S.,
1891 C Brown, Frank F.,
1877 C Brown, Mrs. Lizzie S.,
1877 L Brown, Mrs. Mary E.,
1878 L Brown, Mrs. Sarah H.,
1853 C Bradbury, Mrs. Eliza B., (Hooper) (a)
1884 C Burroughs, Mrs. Anna, (Gregory)   "

1877 L Carleton, Mrs. Hannah H., (Gregory) (a)
1892 C Carr, Walter,   "
1880 L ⎰ Chadwick, Benjamin W.,
1880 L ⎱ Chadwick, Mrs. Stella,
1887 C Chapman, Mrs. Harriet B.,
1898 L Chase, Mrs. Rebecca E.,
1877 L Chinn, Mrs. Eliza P.,
1888 C Chisholm, Mrs. Jane E.,
1877 L Church, Mrs. Hannah H.,
1894 C ⎰ Church, William R.,   (a)
1887 L ⎱ Church, Mrs. Annie M., (Lind) "
1868 C Clothey, Joseph,
1885 C Clough, Mrs. Ella F., (Dinsmore)
1892 C Cole, Mrs. Rebecca, (Usher)
1877 L Collyer, Mrs. Catherine,
1894 C Conway, Ada R.,
1876 L Conway, Mrs. Amanda P.,
1887 C Conway, Florence G.,
1871 C Cross, Hannah R.,   (a)
1849 C Cross, Mary A.,   ·   "
1874 C Courtis, Mrs. Carrie A.,

100

1886 C Dane, Mrs. Mary R., (Stoddard)
1868 C Day, Benjamin,
1878 C Day, Benjamin F.,
1901 L Delano, Mrs. Ellen M.,
1884 C Denning, Mrs. Wilhelmina A.,
1874 C Dinsmore, Hattie,
1894 C Dixey, Martha Ellen,
1877 L Doliber, Mrs. Isabella,

1893 C ⎰ Eastland, Thomas S.,
1893 C ⎱ Eastland, Mrs. Esther E.,
1897 C ⎰ Eustis, Clarence F.,
1890 L ⎱ Eustis, Mrs. Annie,
1898 C Eustis, Charles L.,
1877 L Evans, William T.,

1888 C Felton, Mrs. Mary E.,
1867 C ⎰ Ferguson, Augustus P.,
1857 C ⎱ Ferguson, Caroline E., (Humphrey)
1875 C Florence, Mrs. Emma R.,
1898 L Ford, Lizzie,
1877 L Foss, Ida C.,   (a)
1897 C Foss, Jennie Paine,
1850 C Franks, Mrs. Sarah G.,
1877 C ⎰ Freeto, Frank,
1877 C ⎱ Freeto, Mrs. Frances A., (Haskell)
1885 C ⎰ Freeto, Fred B.,
1901 C ⎱ Freeto, Mrs. Lilian M. S., (McNicholl)
1850 C Freeto, Mrs. Mehitable J., (Rogers)
1876 C Freeto, Philip,

1876 C Frederick, Martha,

1900 C Frost, Abbie Frances,

1894 C Gage, Mrs. Jane H., (Stacey)   (a)

1895 L Gallagher, Joseph W.,   "

1871 C Garney, John G. C.,

1897 C Getchell, Mrs. Lizzie Maria,

1852 L Gile, Mrs. Susan J. D.,   (a)

1895 C Gillis, Mrs. Christie,

1871 C Girdler, Mary Lizzie,

1871 C Glass, Mrs. Mary,

1877 L Goldthwait, Mrs. Mary L.,

1850 C Goodwin, Rebecca T.,

1851 C Goss, Mrs. Martha E., (Kimball)

1877 L Goss, Mrs. Sarah E.,

1877 L { Grant, Deacon Richard T.,

1877 L { Grant, Mrs. Hannah E., (Caswell)

1877 C Graves, Susie D.,

1881 C Greene, Mary A.,

1894 C Gregory, Mrs. Carrie M., (Goldthwait)

1887 L { Gregory, James J. H.,

1877 L { Gregory, Mrs. Lillie S., (Caswell)

1876 C { Gregory, Joseph,

1871 C { Gregory, Mrs. Hannah H., (Pedrick)

1871 C Gregory, Mrs. Sarah E., (Franks)

1866 C Griffith, Mrs. Sarah R.,

1896 L { Hall, Herbert J., M. D.,

1894 C { Hall, Mrs. Eliza P., (Goldthwait)

1876 C Hamelin, Carrie L.,

1892 L Hammond, Mrs. Emma, Died Jan., 1901
1892 L Hammond, Annie B.,
1876 C Hammond, Fred E.,
1877 L Hammond, Mrs. Sebra,
1895 C Hathaway, Mrs. Gertrude M.(Devereaux)
1881 C Hawkes, James W.,
1875 C Hawkes, Mrs. Martha A.,
1885 C Hawkes, Mary J.,
1886 C Hawkes, S. Lizzie,
1885 L Herrick, Mrs. Joanna,
1888 C Holden, Mrs. Alice, (Woolston) (a)
1882 C Homan, Mary E.,
1881 C Humphrey, Caroline E.,
·1874 C Humphrey, Mrs. Hannah H.,
1876 C Humphrey, Mrs. Mary E.,   (a)
1886 C Humphrey, Mrs. Mary Elizabeth,
1885 C Hunt, Mrs. Hattie,
1884 C Hyam, Mary,

1876 C Ingalls, Mrs. Mary H., (Conway)
1859 C Ireson, Susan,

1901 L Johnston, Robert,
1901 L Johnston, Ada S.,

1876 C King, Giles,
1896 C King, Mrs. Sarah W.,
1878 C Knight, Mrs. Caroline,
1871 C Knight, Lizzie M.,
1871 C Knight, Sarah,

1882 C Lancey, Lizzie H.,

1884 C Lemaster, Mrs. Mary E.,

1886 C Lindsey, Amy B.,

1897 C Lindsey, Deliverance B.,

1850 C Lindsey, Mrs. Emily S., (Blaney)

1884 C Lindsey, Mrs. Georgie A., (Martin)

1876 C Lindsey, Mrs. Sarah L.,

1901 C Litchman, Harold B.,

1871 C Litchman, Mrs Sarah,

1850 C Manning, Mrs. Elizabeth W.,

1874 C Martin, Mrs. Hannah B.,

1850 C Martin, Mrs. Mary B., (Hammond) (a)

1876 C Martin, Mrs. Sarah J.,

1901 L Meilbye, James,

1886 C Melzard, Mrs. Mary B.,

1891 C Mitchell, Cora L.,

1877 L Mitchell, Mrs. Elizabeth C.,

1877 L Munroe, Mrs. Marianna,

1875 C North, Mrs. Mary S., (Knowland) (a)

1871 C Neilson, Mrs. Mary A. B., (Harris)

1876 C Oliver, Mrs. Mary E.,

1882 L Parker, Mrs. Annie W.,

1877 L Pedrick, Mrs. Carrie E., (Chapman)

1850 C Pedrick, Mrs. Elizabeth H.,

1874 C Perkins, Mrs. Hannah M.,   (a)

1877 C Pierce, Mrs. Sarah E.,

1871 C Pitman, Mrs. Mary E.,
1877 C ⎰ Pope, George G.,
1876 C ⎱ Pope, Mrs. Carrie A.,
1900 C Potter, Alice Jeannette,
1898 C Potter, Mrs. Lillie, (Foss)
1888 C Power, Mrs. A. Maria,
1886 C Pratt, Lucina H.,

1877 L Ramsdell, Mrs. Carrie C., (Tindley)
1884 C Ramsdell, Mrs. Mary A.,
1884 C Roads, Mrs. Martha D., (Ramsdell)
1884 C Rogers, M. Lizzie,
1897 C Roundey, Mrs. Lizzie M.,
1894 C Rouse, Thomas A.,   (a)
1888 C Russell, Hattie,

1852 L Sanborn, Nathan Perkins,
1876 C Savory, Abbie B.,
1900 C Savory, Arthur Frank,
1855 C Savory, Mrs. Hannah,
1877 L ⎰ Savory, Deacon Benjamin,
1874 C ⎱ Savory, Mrs. Sarah E., (Harrington)
1885 C ⎰ Shattuck, Charles H.,
1885 L ⎱ Shattuck, Mrs. Ellen,
1885 C Shepard, Annie,
1897 C Smethurst, Jennie Bessom,
1871 C Smethurst, Lizzie T.,
1863 L Smethurst, Mrs. Mary J.,
1874 C Smith, Mrs. Mary E.,

1877 L { Stacey, Girdler,
1877 L { Stacey, Mrs. Annie B.,
1858 C Stacey, William,   (a)
1858 C Standley, Mrs. Eliza, (Broughton)
1858 C Stevens, Mrs. Harriet H.,
1896 L Stewart, Mrs. Pansy,   (a)
1898 C { Stone, Andrew M.,
1898 C { Stone, Mrs. Eleanor P., (Chamberlin)
1861 L Stone, Mrs. Ruth A.,
1842 C Stone, Mrs. Priscilla W.,
1886 L Stoddard, Carrie E.,
1886 L Stoddard, Samuel P.,
1888 L { Sumner, J. F.,   (a)
1888 L { Sumner, Mrs. Mary L.,   "
1888 L Sumner, Lottie M.,
1888 L Sumner, Maggie L.,
1876 C Sweet, Mrs. Elizabeth E.,
1884 C Symonds, Annie B.,

1876 C Thompson, Lizzie,
1877 L Tindley, Mrs. Margaret,
1898 L { True, Dr. Richard S.,
1898 L { True, Mrs. Thankful E.,
1898 L True, Harry E.,
1898 L True, J. Webster,
1898 L True, Richard S., Jr.,
1898 L True, Charlotte L.,
1898 L True, Margaret P.,
1885 C { Tutt, Deacon Edward D.,
1884 C { Tutt, Mrs. Sarah W., (Main)

1884 C Tutt, Hannah,
1874 C Tutt, Mrs. Hannah A.,
1879 C Tutt, Mrs. Mary Abbie, (Eastland)
1889 C ⎰ Tutt, Deacon Richard,
1883 C ⎱ Tutt, Mrs. Annie C., (Woolston)

1877 L Usher, Mrs. Hattie,
1886 C Usher, Mrs. Mattie, (Broughton)

1877 L Washburn, Mrs. Sarah,
1900 C Wayland, Frederick,   (a)
1900 C ⎰ Wayland, Valentine,   "
1900 C ⎱ Wayland, Mrs. Alice
1877 L West, Mrs. Lizzie E., (Savory)
1836 C White, Susan H.,
1877 L Woodfin, Mrs. Margaret A.,
1888 C Woolston, Ellen E.,
1885 C Woolston, William G.,

March 18, 1901.